T

SECRET PLACE OF PRAYER

SAM PERCY AGYEMFRA

THE SECRET PLACE OF PRAYER

ISBN: 9798763252446

Edited by Winnie Annie-Adjei, Terry Downs and Dr. Julia Roberts

Cover & Book Design: 40k Designs, www.fortyk.com

CONTENTS

ACKNOWLEDGEMENTS

This book was made possible through the love, prayers and support of my family and special friends. First of all, I want to thank the Lord for helping me do something I thought was impossible; write a book. From the foundation of my faith, the Lord has taught me about the secret place of prayer and how to write about it.

This book would not have been written without the wisdom, knowledge and understanding of the Word of God through the Holy Spirit and with the help of my spiritual mentor Bishop N. A. Tackie-Yarboi from Victory Bible Church International Worldwide and also having been under the ministry of Pastor Colin Dye the Senior Pastor of Kensington Temple Church, London, UK; Reverend Edward Kwadwo Agyemfra, IGCC Kokomlemle Branch, Accra, Ghana; Pastor Timothy Akinluyi of Kings Church, London, UK and of course, my precious wife Adelaide, always supporting me with her prayers.

INTRODUCTION

The secret place of prayer might seem to be an unusual title for a book on prayer. It was derived from Genesis 4:26, which states: "**Seth also had a son, and he named him Enoch. At that time men began to call on the name of the Lord**" Call on the name of the LORD means that prayer and worship of God began in this era and also **Psalm 91:1 which reads "He that dwells in the secret place of the most high (Jehovah- Elyon) will rest in the shadow of the Almighty" (Jehovah El- Shaddai).**

The need to pray seems to be built in the heart of every human being, and it is the person "who dwells in the secret place of prayer" and abides under God's shadow who will experience intimacy and a supernatural lifestyle.

In the secret place of prayer is the supernatural favour of God released from heaven. It can create life from death and can change an unrighteous life to one of righteousness. It restores health from sickness, brings victory rather than defeat, and creates success rather than failure. It brings encouragement and not despair, propels your faith rather than your fear, bringing prosperity rather than poverty to one's life, to families, society and to nations. Therefore, if we obey and do what God has commanded in His Holy Book, The Bible, we will see some of the benefits of prayer which are laid out in Deuteronomy 28:1-14.

To dwell in the secret place reveals the benefit of time spent in God's presence. In Psalm 91, we were not told where the secret place is, but we discover what God desires to do in our encounter with him in the secret place and how He wants to bless or reward us simply for being in the secret place and in our obedience to him. We also discover that "in the secret place" He is able to reveal himself in our lives.

Jesus himself did tell us where the secret place is when his disciples asked him to teach them how to pray. Commonly referred to as The Lord's Prayer in (Matthew 6:6-14) and (Luke 11:1-4), especially Matthew 6:6 Jesus goes on in detail about the "where" and "how" of the secret place. 'But when you pray, go into your room, close the door and pray to your Father, who is unseen. Then your Father, who sees what is done in secret will reward you.'

Prayer is not changing the will of God but changing our will to conform to God's will.

Prayer is simply a form of communication with your heavenly Father God and God talking back to you His child, just as you would communicate with someone you know intimately.

INTRODUCTION

Prayer is not just words: It is communicating with God. It is our spirit making live contact with God's Spirit. Through prayer, we come to know who the all-powerful, all loving God is, allowing and permitting Him to direct our lives the best way. Through prayer you can call the forces of heaven into any situation, anywhere, anytime, for anybody. There is no distance in prayer.

Prayer shapes our lives: In prayer, we expose ourselves to God's light and sunbathe in the warmth of divine love. We absorb His goodness. His light also penetrates to the core of our existence. God knows and has a purpose why we should dwell in His shelter. It is life from above. Through prayer, we allow God to direct our lives more than we can imagine.

To be able to dwell and be with somebody you would need to communicate sincerely and be transparent and have intimacy with the person, always wanting to commune with them and to be in their presence. This process is called prayer. In this way prayer is not working to change our Father's mind, but it is instead finding the mind of God.

Prayer is a daily necessity: Through prayer and abiding in God's presence, He gives you rest, and you receive the rest He has purposed for you because you are in His presence, and He is pouring himself out to you.

Prayer is also an opportunity to receive from our heavenly Father all that He desire to give us daily.

Sometimes God moves sovereignly, giving you neither notice nor explanation. Other times He moves only in answer to prayers. What begins in heaven returns to heaven, via the mysterious power of prayer. In this way prayer is not working to change our Father's mind but it is instead finding the mind of God.

The Lord's teaching on prayer in Matthew 6: 5-13 with a shorter version in Luke 21:2-4 is commonly known as The Lord's Prayer. There have been lots of misconceptions not only among believing Christians but also the worldwide audience on questions such as: What prayer is? Who should we or do we pray too? When to pray? Where to pray? How to pray, what length of prayer is right and even what position to adopt when praying.

It is my prayer that this book, with the help of the Holy Spirit, will enlighten your understanding of prayer from the book of Genesis, from the model of Jesus's prayer and even from Paul's letters to the churches in the New Testament. I pray that you will be inspired to have a desire, a discipline and a delight for prayer.

FOREWORD

Many Christians attend church year by year, copy what they see others do in terms of praying and then this imitation becomes a central part of their lives. However, at the back of their mind they are wondering, is this it? Is this all there is to praying? Everybody prays, even unbelievers.

For us to be victorious Christians living the victorious life, we need to be taught how and why to pray. We need to be taught effective ways of praying that will bring results.

I have been praying for years but with no results. No change in my marriage, home, sickness ..." so emptiness has invaded their souls because of lack of understanding. James 4:2 says. "You do not have because you do not ask. You ask and do not receive, because you ask amiss..."

We all know we need to pray, but how? Many people pray for one thing and then say, with their own words, the opposite of what was just prayed.

Jesus was a source of continuous admiration to his own

disciples. Life with him was an awesome experience of joy and incomprehension. The disciples had travelled with him the length and breadth of the land of Israel. They had seen inroads made into the darkening powers of sickness, death, and despair throughout the land. The disciples could not forget the mighty demonstrations of Jesus's power.

They also remembered those who were lame, blind, sick, dumb, deaf and afflicted... who had been healed, set free and sent back to their loved ones.

The disciples were continually dumbfounded at the wisdom that Jesus manifested. They were forever watching him at a distance, wondering, what was the secret of his wisdom and power.

Take note of Luke 11:1. Now it came to pass, as Jesus was praying in a certain place, that when he ceased, one of His disciples said to Him, "Lord, teach us to pray, as John also taught his disciples."

The disciples were watching Jesus in prayer and, as they watched, it dawned in the heart of one of the disciples, unnamed, that somehow the amazing power that Jesus had was connected with his prayer life. When Jesus had finished, one of them, speaking for all the disciples, said to him, "Lord, teach us to pray."

Notice this disciplined follower of the Lord, requested that Jesus teach him how to pray and he even reminded Jesus that

John taught his disciples how to pray.

Therefore, if John taught his disciples how to pray, then the disciples of Jesus should ask Jesus how they should pray.

In other words they were saying, "Some of us were once John's disciples and we were taught by him how to pray, but Lord, we have been watching you, and we see that you are a master at prayer. Now as John once taught us how to pray, would you also impart to us the secrets of prayer? For, as we have been watching you, we have seen that in some manner, the marvel and mystery of your character is linked with your prayer life, and it has made us aware of how little we really know about prayer. Lord, would you teach us to pray?"

We all need to learn how to pray. There is a tendency that leaders and pastors assume that people know how to pray. This is not always the case and presents a challenge to Christians growing in their prayer life.

Prayer is intended to produce right results in our lives.

Therefore, in this book you will learn principles and instructions about prayer and your Journey Starts Here.

Pastor Wilson Wasswa Lubega

It has been my privilege to know Sam Percy Agyemfra as a fellow minister and a dear brother for many years.

We are living in unprecedented times where there is a great need for believers to pray.

In this book Pastor Sam brings a timely and much needed message to the body of Christ. He re-emphasises the principles of prayer and the importance of returning to the secret place, to labour for our churches, families, our communities and our nations to birth God's agenda in the earth.

This is a must-read book for every believer who desires to be in partnership with God through prayer.

Reverend Nat Mantey

CHAPTER 1

A CALL TO PRAYER

At the beginning of my new life in Christ in the early 1980s, between 3am to 4am in my room, I would be awakened with a deep desire to pray and call on the name of the Lord. This experience lasted for about one or two hours as the Holy Spirit urged me, inspired me, prompted and led me to pray. With the Holy Spirit led desire to reading the word of God, I was able to build on my prayer life with my heavenly Father.

God created a desire in the heart of men to call on the name of the Lord after the fall of man in the beginning of Genesis. The bible says that men began to call on the name of the Lord. (Genesis 4:26)., after their disobedience had caused banishment from the Garden of Eden.

The word of God came through King Solomon in (2 Chronicles 7: 14) directing the people of God what they should do in order for them to hear from heaven. The Bible states, "If my people who are called by my name, will humble themselves, pray and seek my face and turn from their wicked ways, then I will hear from heaven and will forgive their sin and heal their land.

Prayer is a foundational pillar to your individual Christian life, also to the life of your family and the ministry of your church, society and nation. Like a proper foundation that secures a building, prayer gives you something trustworthy on which to rest. It is clear as to why Satan works overtime to keep you busy and distracted so that you lose regular in-depth communication with your heavenly Father.

I believe that God is calling the universal Church to pray. We must make our voice heard in heaven. We usually make our voices heard on earth, through social media, digitals, telephone. What about making our voices heard in heaven?

For many Christians prayer is a lost art and the desire to pray has gone. This desire to pray has to be originated by the Holy Spirit in our heart, which can only happen when we are close to God's word.

I believe that when we pray, humanity cooperates with divinity. More things are accomplished by prayer than we can dream of.

Our heavenly Father expects us to call on Him and He will answer us and show us great and unsearchable things we do not know. He is ever ready to hear from us. (Jeremiah 33:3).

It is God's desire for those he has created to call on Him. He is expecting our response on earth to call him because He has given us the right to do that on earth. He is ever ready to listen and answer us if we pray and seek Him with a sincere heart as promised to Jeremiah (29:12, 13). Once again, the Lord God promises in His word that before we call, He will answer and while we are still speaking He will hear (Isaiah 65:24). The Lord is faithful to His word and is seeking His people to call and communicate with Him regularly.

I believe that in order to attain an open heaven in our situations and the salvation of souls, we need to be engaged in fervent and active prayers. Nothing happens by chance. In Luke 3:21, 23 during Jesus' baptism, as He was praying, heaven was opened, and the Holy Spirit descended on Him in a bodily form like a dove. Verse 23 states that, a voice came from heaven "affirming that" You are my son, whom I love, with you I am well pleased. All favour, grace and truth was showered on him. We can see that, the Father provided Jesus him with power and confirmed His love for him.

If you allow prayer to become your primary emphasis, that divine progression will be manifested in you as the Holy Spirit brings His purity. Furthermore, His ministry of prayer, His power and perfected praise will be shown in your life. There is a lesson we can learn from Jesus when he entered the temple in (Matthew 21:12-16), Jesus entered the temple area and drove out all who were buying and selling there. He overturned the tables of the money changers and the benches of those selling doves. He declared to them, "My house will be called a house of prayer, but you have made it into a den of robbers". The blind and the lame came to him at the temple, and he healed them. The chief priests and the teachers saw the wonderful things He did and also the children were shouting in the temple area, Hosanna to the son of David, they were indignant. Observe the progression of prayer in the verses.

Firstly, in verse 12 - He cleansed the temple, and it became a house of Purity.

Secondly in verse 13 - He announced that His house is a house of prayer, and it should be recognised as this. As it was also prophesied by Isaiah in Isaiah 56:7 that His house will be called a house of prayer for all nations. In verse 14, the blind and the lame came, and Jesus healed them, it now also became a house of power. In verse 15, the children saw the marvellous things He had done in the temple and began to shout Hosanna to the son of David. Finally, after the temple became a house of power it was transformed to a house of praise. These are steps used by Jesus to transform the temple into a house of prayer as God intended it to be. (Purity, Prayer, Power, Praise)

If our body is the temple of the Holy Spirit, (1 Corinthians 6:19), then Paul's profound statement in 1 Corinthians 6:19 "Do you not know that your body is the temple of the Holy Spirit, who is in you, whom you have received from God? You are not your own." will hold true. This means that if you are the temple of God today, you could be, transformed into a house of purity to become a house of prayer, power, and praise. I believe there are three places that are meant to be "house of prayer":

1. Ourselves. As temples of the Holy Spirit, we ourselves can become house of prayer.
2. Our homes can become houses of prayer.
3. Our Churches can become houses of prayer.

Our reasonable service is to present our bodies as a living sacrifice, holy and acceptable to God. (Romans 12:1) Also one of the reasonable services to God is our prayers.

As stated previously in Isaiah 56:7 the Bible tells us that "His house shall be called a house of prayer for all nations". Prayer and evangelism go together. Without prayer, reaching the hearts of people who are lost, or the nations will be difficult and at most delayed.

CHAPTER 2

THE PURPOSE OF PRAYER

A scripture in Isaiah (Isaiah 14:24) assures us that The Lord almighty has sworn, that He does have a plan, so it will stand. The plan and purpose of God stands, as confirmed in Proverbs 16:1-3- "To man belongs the plan of the heart but from the Lord comes the reply of the tongue. All of a man's ways seem innocent to him, but motives are weighed by the Lord."

Verse 3 of Proverbs 16 tells us to commit to the Lord whatever we do and our plans will succeed. One of the reasons why God created us, is to worship Him (John 4:23) and to have a relationship with Him by means of communicating with Him in prayer.

You can strengthen your relationship with God by communicating frequently with Him through prayer. You can learn of His preference, His plan for your life and His activity in the world by prayer. That is how He can fulfil His plan and purpose on earth through us.

Too often we view prayers as transactional, we pray only when we need God's help with a specific problem; for example, a loved one becomes ill, a marriage breakdown, a financial loss or death in the family. While God certainly hears these prayer requests, His greatest desire is to have ongoing, consistent fellowship with us through prayer.

Romans 8:29 states, "those God foreknew He also predestined to be conformed to His likeness." When you read the preceding verses in this chapter, you discover that one of the ways God does this is through prayer.

This should encourage you to pray. Many times, we do not pray because we do not think anything is happening! But with God something is always happening. He is always working when it comes to prayer. He is either answering the way you hope or changing your heart through the Spirit's intercession to bring your prayer into harmony with His will. 'But you say, I do not see anything happening'. When you plant a seed, you do not come back the next day expecting green shoots and leaves. Does that mean nothing is happening? No! A host of necessary processes are taking place below the ground where you cannot see. Do not make the mistake of thinking that because you do not see the evidence, that nothing is happening.

It is not harvest time yet. One way in which God is making us more like Jesus is by helping us to pray the way Jesus prayed. Not my will but Thine will be done. (Luke 22:42). That means when your prayer lines up with His will. He is already working on it even though you cannot see it. If your prayer is not in accordance with His will, He is working to change your request by changing you. It is His will to make you more like Jesus through prayers. That is His purpose for you in prayer.

We are also reminded by King Solomon in Proverbs 19:2 that many are the plans in a man's heart, but it is the Lord's purpose that prevails. What is in line with His will and purpose is what will prevail.

Notice in Psalm 33:10, that, "The Lord [foils] the plans of the nations. He [thwarts] the purpose of the people" But in Psalm 33:11, we are told that the plan of the Lord stands firm forever and the purposes of His heart through all generations will prevail. It is up to us, by the help of the Holy Spirit through prayers, for His plans and purposes to be revealed to us in His written word and in our renewed inner Spirit. I believe prayer is the key to unveil this to us.

From these scriptures, we can understand that God is a God of purpose. He has a purpose for everything that He has created and also said that it is only God's purpose that will stand forever.

Prayer, which is God's breath (communicating to God) for the believer, is one of His purposes that will stand forever.

Jesus states in Luke 18:1 Men ought always to pray and not too faint. In Paul's 1st letter to the church at Thessalonica (1 Thessalonians 5:17), Paul encouraged the church to pray without ceasing.

Prayer releases the supernatural of God's hand and favour from heaven to us. God knows and controls everything. When you think of renouncing your will and embracing the will of God, let me suggest you bear three truth in mind. First of all, God loves you more than you love yourself. Secondly, God understand you better than you understand yourself. And thirdly, God want only the best for you. When you truly yield to God's will, you will discover that it is what the Bible says it is: "good and acceptable and perfect" (Romans 12:2). It is His purpose to change situations when we surrender our lives and pray. All of these can be manifested through our intense prayers. If you stop praying, heaven shuts down as we are informed in Matthew 18:19.

Nothing will happen on earth without mankind's cooperation. Even though God is a Sovereign God who can do everything except that He cannot sin, lie, or repent, it is the believer's legal authority on earth to pray and have a connection with God asking for heaven to come down to earth according to His will and purpose.

CHAPTER 3

PRAYER AS A TOP PRIORITY

"But seek first the kingdom of God and His righteousness, and all these things will be added unto you". Jesus said in Matthew 6:33.

I have heard it said that "the first 10 or 30 minutes of each day really determines how your day will go". If you begin your day in prayer, acknowledging God as first in your life, you are making a wise choice.

Prayer is the most important event in our life, and we need to prioritise it. It has to be continuous, reoccurring and consistent. Too often, rather than putting Jesus first in our life, we allow many thoughts and things to consume us.

Scripture reminds us that anything we love more, serve more or worship more than Jesus himself is idolatry, plain and simple! Jesus will not share His place in our lives. So, before you pray, before you start asking, make sure you are practicing the principle of putting God first (seeking His face and communicating with him) about all areas of your life.

I know life can be busy. I know obligations must be met. I'm suggesting that before we tend to our responsibilities, we should devote ourselves to God in prayer. I need that and so do you.

Each of us needs a set-aside, set-apart solitude with the Living God at key moments throughout our day in order to navigate this journey called life, There can be no answered prayers until we're willing to spend time kneeling before God to receive His mind for us, and what He delights and desires to do for us and give to us. Keeping our focus on God through prayer, reaps great rewards.

Prayer is an essential tactic if we want to walk in victory in our own lives and see that the gospel of Christ is made known on the earth and in the lives of people.

Paul in training Timothy for the ministry, wanted him to understand how the church works. So he began with the most important stuff, prayer.

In a nutshell, Paul was saying that before you do anything else, pray; before you teach anybody else, pray; before you make decisions, pray. Why? Because if God is not on your side, you will not succeed. Most of us do understand this intellectually and with head knowledge.

We say a quick prayer as we are running out of the door, we say grace before a meal, and we open our church services with prayer. But few of us grasp the real importance and intention of prayer and Paul does not want Timothy to be misled or misinformed about the place of prayer in the church.

We dare not fool ourselves into thinking that we 'can make things happen' without prayer. Continuing effective prayers of faith always produce results. That is why Jesus commanded and encouraged us in Luke 18:1 that men ought always to pray and not too faint or give up. Paul again encouraged Timothy and the universal church in 1 Timothy 2:8 that all men everywhere were to lift up Holy hands in prayer.

Prayer is one of the weapons of our warfare to combat and defeat the work of the devil in our Christian walk with God. The Bible tells us in 2 Corinthians 10:4-5 that the weapons of our warfare are not carnal, but mighty through God to the pulling down of strongholds; casting down imaginations and everything that exalts itself against the knowledge of God and bringing into captivity every thought to the obedience of Christ.

Every Christian must be involved in spiritual warfare, because we are constantly engaged in spiritual battles with the affairs of the devil (Ephesians 6:12).

We have to win the battle on our knees. Even though the battle belongs to the Lord and the victory is ours

CHAPTER 4

DIFFERENT KINDS OF PRAYERS

There are five main forms of prayer, and they are praise, petition, supplication, intercession and thanksgiving. However, in scripture you can find different kind of prayers and the majority of these will be comprised of the five forms of prayers above.

There are different kinds of prayers in the word of God, and they all follow the same model of Jesus's teaching about prayer in Matthew 6:9-13. Paul also urged us in Ephesians 6:18 "To pray in the spirit on all occasions with all kinds of prayers and requests. With this in mind, be alert and always keep on praying for all the saints". He also reminded us about different kinds of prayers in 1st Timothy 2:1 He urged us that, first of all, requests, prayers, intercession and thanksgiving be made for everyone. The Bible encourages and urges us to use different kinds of prayers depending on the situation at any given time, and how the Spirit of God is leading you.

DIFFERENT KINDS OF PRAYERS

These are some of the different kinds of prayers that are in the Bible.

Prayer of Adoration

Prayer of Confession

Prayer of Thanksgiving

Prayer of Supplication

Prayer of Petition

Prayer of Intercession

Prayer of Wrestling

Prayer of Communion

Prayer of Praise

Prayer of Worship

Prayer of Declaration/Proclamation

Prayer of Command

Prayer of Binding and Losing

Prayer of Agreement

Prayer of Repentance

Prayer of Victory

Prayer of Dedication

Prayer of Commitment

Prayer of Surrender

Praying Scriptures

Prophetic Prayer

Prevailing Prayer

Warring and Travailing Prayer

Persistence Prayer

Loud Prayer

Silent Prayer

Imprecation/Judgmental Prayer.

PRAYER OF ADORATION:

As you approach God, confessing your sins and presenting yourself to Him to petition, you enter a period of divine adoration. Take time in your prayer life to "Give unto the Lord the glory due to His name, worship the Lord in the beauty of holiness" (Psalm 29:2). This intimate worship and adoration can only be expressed from your heart or perhaps in a heavenly language. This is more than telling God who He is. By using most of His names and characteristics, you are conveying the deep love that you have for the Father, loving the Lord in His presence, loving him back for His love for you. This is where you rest in his bosom, with all humility in His majesty and glory.

PRAYER OF CONFESSION:

How do you approach the presence of God? You start by confessing and declaring three things:

1. Confession of your sins
2. Who God is
3. Who you are in Christ

You can start by confessing your sins before God, anything in your life that displeases God either by thought, deed or action and believe that God is faithful and just to forgive you and to cleanse you from all unrighteousness, according to 1John 1:9. Continue by saying who God is as described in His word, for example God is Love, a forgiving God, He is faithful, Alpha and Omega, Healer, Saviour, Provider and Shepherd. Now begin to declare His promises. Lord your word declares that 'you are faithful and just to forgive us and cleanse us from all unrighteousness'' You can declare God's promises in Zachariah 13:9 "they shall call upon my name, and I will hear them." Also, you can confess who you are in Christ. For example, I am a child of God as it says in your word that, as many as received you, you gave them power to become the children of God, (John 1:12). I am saved (Romans 5:8-10, Ephesians 2:1-10).

I am loved (1 John 3:16, Romans 5:5) I am a new person in Christ Jesus (2 Corinthians 5:17) Also, I am chosen by God. (Romans 8:30, Ephesians 1: 4) I am blessed in the heavenly places with all spiritual blessings in Christ Jesus. (Ephesians 1:3). I have been adopted as a child of God to the family of God (Ephesians 5), and many more. You may ask, why should I quote or confess scriptures? After all, God already knows. Of course, when you say them, you align yourself with the word of God and you make them your own. As you begin to confess the promises of God, you lose sight of yourself in humility as you tell him that He is God Almighty, and you are His child.

PRAYER OF THANKSGIVING:

This is when you are walking in the path of prayer with thanksgiving in your heart to God. You have gratitude and appreciation in your heart for what He has done for you and others in the past, present and future through the power of the cross. Continual thanksgiving should be on your lips all day long whether you are at home, in Church, driving, working or spending time with the family. Your heart and mind should be filled with God's goodness and mercy. David also encouraged us in the book of Psalms to make sacrifices of thanksgiving to God, fulfilling our vows to the highest God. And when we call on him in the day of trouble, he delivers us, and He will honour us. Before we come to God's presence, we have to come with thanksgiving and praise (Psalms 100:4 paraphrased and Psalms 95:2). We do have Paul's instruction that we are not only to be established in the faith but abounding therein with thanksgiving to God. It is not enough to just pray, without also being patient and giving thanks to God. Thanksgiving is the highest form of prayer as God appreciates it when we are grateful for what He has done for us and others, and what He is about to do. This shows that His love for you is not seen as vain or something to be trampled on. Believing, giving thanks and continuing in prayer until you obtain an answer from God. Also believe that God does hear us and will answer our prayers (1 Chronicles 16:8-36) and (Psalm 136:1-26). In all circumstances give thanks, for this is the will of God in Christ Jesus concerning you (1 Thessalonians 5:18). God wants us to give Him thanks during our prayers, as we paraphrase Philippians 4:6 "In everything by prayer and petition, with thanksgiving, present your request to God." Let's look at some examples of Paul's prayer of thanksgiving. He always gave thanks to God during his prayers for the churches and encourages us to do the same (Ephesians 1:15-16), (Philippians 1:3-4), (Colossians 1:3, 4:2), (1 Thessalonians 1:2), 1 Thessalonians 5.16-18), (2 Thessalonians 2:13,14), (1 Timothy 1:12-13), Philemon 1:4-6). Thankfulness to God benefits us as it provides defence against the temptation of sin (Ephesians 5:3-5). It helps us to build our confidence in God, which will be richly rewarded rather than throwing it away. (Hebrews 12:35)

PRAYER OF SUPPLICATION:

In supplication, we not only declare the sovereignty of God and our place as believers, but confess other people's needs as well as our own needs to Him. Apostle Paul encourages us to put on the whole armour of God. Also, he urged us to pray with all prayers and supplication in the spirit, being alert and watching and praying for all the saints (Ephesians 6:18). Furthermore, supplication means that you pray and put yourself in place of others, praying for them in their situations. We need to present their requests to God. Although God knows their petitions before we even ask, He is waiting to hear from us before He acts. Even though He is sovereign God, He still wants us to be specific, tenacious and full of faith when in prayer for others and he will be attentive to our prayers (1 Peter 3:12 and Mark 11:24). Unfortunately, many people do not understand that there is a lot more for prayers to be effective. They often end their time of prayer when they finish saying, "bless me Lord and this is my list of requests."

PRAYER OF PETITION:

The channel that most people mean when they talk about "prayer" is petition, asking for physical and material needs to be met. But remember: Praying is not just thinking of anything we want and asking for it. Praying is discovering God's revealed purpose in Scripture, and then praying for the outworking of that purpose. Looking at (1 John 5:14-15) Now this is the confidence that we have in Him, that if we ask anything according to His will, He hear us. And if we know that He hears us, whatever we ask, we know that we have the petitions that we have ask of Him. This is petition- asking for thing. One of the secrets of getting things from God is receiving. Jesus in (Matthew 16:24) told his disciples that "Until now you have not asked anything in my name. Ask and you will receive, and your joy will be complete. Our Lord Jesus want us to bring our petitions to him. It is not only asking that is important but asking and receiving.

PRAYER OF INTERCESSION:

From the time of Moses through to the monarchy, with certain kinds of prayers, the emphasis was on intercession (Abraham: Genesis 18:22 Moses: Exodus 32:11ff; Samuel: 1 Samuel 7:5ff; Solomon: 1 Kings 8:22ff; Hezekiah: 2 Kings 19:14ff).

This is the point whereby God wants us to pray and stand in the gap for someone, for family, for others, for our workplaces, your church, for Church Leaders, for other churches, your city and for nations. God spoke through the prophet Ezekiel when he wrote, "I looked for a man among them (the people of Jerusalem) who would make a hedge and stand in the gap before me on behalf of the land, that I should not destroy it but I found no-one." (Ezekiel 22:30) The gap is the distance between what is and what can be. And when there is a gap in someone's life, in a family, in a church, in a city, or in a relationship with God, due to a particular sin or sins, as a believer you have the privilege and responsibility of placing yourself in the gap and praying for them. This time, you declare and put God's hedge of protection on you and from the work of the Devil, pleading and interceding on their behalf before God to confess, repent of their sins (Ezekiel 22:30-31). During this time of intercession, God can speak to us, show us pictures, or bring faces and names to our hearts and mind. You sense an inner urge to pray for someone or for the above topics mentioned, although sometimes you may not even know what or why you are praying.

Paul wrote in Romans 8:26 "Likewise the Spirit also helps our infirmities, for we know not what we should pray for as we ought, but the Spirit itself makes intercession for us with groans which cannot be uttered". Intercession is where spiritual breakthroughs occur. It can happen by taking each of the above steps already discussed. Your heart should be prepared for effective prayers and should be ready to talk to God on this level of intercession. Remember, (Acts 12:5) the church was praying earnestly for Peter when he was in prison. Suddenly he was set free and was helped to escape by an angel of the Lord. This signifies intense intercessory prayer by the church. Many of the victories that we celebrate in the open are first won by such intercession in the secret place. It is a specialised ministry and God could be calling you into it. Prayer of Intercession can be individual or corporate. Jesus Christ who is at the right hand of God is also interceding for us to become the fullness of God (Romans 8:34). (1st Timothy 2:1) Apostle Paul here urges Christians that most importantly, "requests, prayers, **intercession** and thanksgiving should be made for everyone". (All people whatever is their background, race, culture, nationality, and whatever creed they read) this includes Kings and all who are in authority, "that we may live peaceful and quiet lives in all godliness and holiness". It continues to say this is good and pleases God our Saviour. Who wants all men to be saved and come to the knowledge of the truth.

PRAYER OF WRESTLING:

This kind of prayer is like having a combat fight against every strategy you see the enemy is using against the people of God. You can wrestle in prayer, before God, in the things that the devil is using to hinder your communication and walk with God and also wrestle in prayer for others. In the book of Colossians (Colossians 4:12), Paul made mention of one of their members Epaphras, a servant of Jesus Christ who was always wrestling in prayer for the Church in Colossae that they may stand firm in all the will of God, be matured and fully assured. This type of prayer is so strenuous that it becomes agonising. Agonising in prayer is for a limited time only. Epaphras wrestled and agonised again and again as he prayed for his beloved brothers and sisters. When Jesus agonised in the Garden of Gethsemane, it was for a period of about three hours. Wrestling before God against every strategy or plan of the devil makes an impact in God's kingdom. However, do not wrestle with God but do not give up until victory is won. Some kinds of blessing cannot be achieved except by wrestling in prayer. If you wrestle with God like what Jacob did in Genesis 32:22-31, simply because God is working in a way that does not meet your approval, you force Him to put you out of joint.

When you want to wrestle in prayers these are a few things that you should consider, do not accept defeat, build your faith, remove any roadblocks or hindrances to your prayer, break yourself free from any sin that controls you with the help of the Holy Spirit, and rely on God's strength.

PRAYER OF COMMUNION:

This is where prayers are no longer words. True prayers come from the heart and are based upon relationship. They are the language of heaven, the avenue by which you enter the throne room of heaven and commune with your heart to your loving heavenly father.

Have you ever looked at your spouse or loved one and expressed your love without saying a word? At times there is no need to say, "I love you". This is what will start to transpire when you commune with the Holy Spirit through Jesus to the Father. It will develop, but not until you have taken a step which will lead to such a moment. It happens after you have released yourself from any spirit of heaviness within your spirit, and after you have worshipped the Lord. This brings the freedom necessary for you to sincerely communicate with your heavenly Father. The apostle Paul prayed "The grace of our Lord Jesus Christ and the love of God, and the communion of the Holy Spirit, be with you all" (2 Corinthians 13:14). Communion is the key. It takes time and there are no short cuts.

PRAYER OF PRAISE:

This is where you use praise as a form of prayer, using God's praises, singing songs to praise him for what He is doing or is about to do. Also, to praise him through your situation or what He has already done.

By faith you should know that a miracle is on the way. You should praise God for it and see it by faith (Mark 11:24). Then comes a time of refreshing and praise when you begin to celebrate what God has done and has promised to do. Like the psalmist (David), you lift your hands and shout "Praise the Lord for the Lord is good: sing praises unto his name" (Psalm 135:3), and I will praise thee with my whole heart (Psalm138:1). Praise the Lord, O my soul. I will praise the Lord all my life; I will sing praise to my God as long as I live. (Psalms 146:1-2). The walls of Jericho tumbled down when the people of Israel praised God and marched around the city for six days and then on the seventh day, marched around it for seven times. Joshua and the people of Israel celebrated the victory by praising God before the wall of Jericho fell down and after they had overcome and conquered (Joshua 6:12-20). There is power in our praises, and we should give praises to God before, during and after any crisis in our life. It helps us to focus on Him and not on ourselves in times of difficult situations and crisis and when we are not even in trouble, we should praise Him.

PRAYER OF WORSHIP:

This form of prayer is where you worship the Lord and ponder over the words of God which have been used in the worship songs in your heart to God. Worshipping God through His word in songs is also a form of prayer to God. This form of prayer releases healing, deliverance and salvation and it also gives us answers as children of God. God desires us to worship Him in Spirit and in truth (John 4:24). Being in the atmosphere of worship, by the power of the Holy Spirit and the word of God, brings us closer to God in our prayers. He also urges us in Psalm 96:9 to worship Him in the beauty of holiness.

PRAYER OF DECLARATION/PROCLAMATIONS:

Prayers of declaration happens when you take God's covenant promises in the word of God and declare them to be in line with your word over yourself, your family, your church, your work and your situations. We see an example of this (Nehemiah 9:5-37) after Nehemiah led the Israelites to confess their sins and the wickedness of their fathers to God. Nehemiah then started to declare and affirm God's covenant promises over the people of Israel.

PRAYER OF COMMAND:

Prayers of command are not familiar with the majority of Christians. However in situations where the enemy has taken a stronghold, depending on discernment of the Holy Spirit, God has given us the authority to command any power of darkness to be cast out, destroyed, evil spirits to leave, demons to be cast out (Mark 16:17) and people to be set free from their bondage through the name of Jesus. For example, in Matthew 17:14-19 Jesus rebuked a demon from a boy and healed him of seizures. Jesus also drove out an evil spirit from a man who had been possessed with demons (Mark 1:21-27). He again cast out an evil spirit from a demon possessed man who lived among the tombs (Mark 5:1-8). This was all done by a word of command from Jesus. These are not quite prayers but instead, they are prayers of command using the authority in Him. As believers we can also use the same authority that Jesus has given to us.

In Mark 16:17 Jesus instructed believers to cast out demons in His name. In Mark 4:39 Jesus rebuked the wind and commanded the waves to be quiet. I believe that sometimes we need to express an authority of command in our prayers if necessary. We notice that in the book of Acts (Acts 16:16-19), Paul encountered a slave girl who had a spirit of divination. He commanded the spirit to come out of her, in the name of Jesus, and immediately the spirit left her.

PRAYER OF BINDING & LOSING:

A promise given by Jesus in Matthew 16:19 when Jesus said to Peter that his revelation and acknowledgement on Him (Jesus) That, He was the Son of the Living God. Jesus replied in saying that upon this rock Jesus will build his church and the Gates of Hell cannot prevail against it. Scripture says in Matthew 16:19 that Jesus promises to give believers the keys to the kingdom of heaven. Therefore, whatever we bind on earth will be bound in heaven and whatever we loose on earth will be loosed in heaven. Jesus is referring to binding and loosing as the keys to the Kingdom and we have to know how to use these keys of the kingdom.

Jesus says that "whatever you bind on earth will be bound in heaven and whatever we lose on earth will be loosed in the heavenly realm". Binding is like a spiritual handcuff. You can bind a demon, but you cannot bind a person's will. It is like tying up something with a chain or rope. Binding is not the same as casting out demons. Casting out demons is a permanent result, while binding is to tire them for a period of time. God instructs and authorises us to bind the works of the enemy on earth and to loose those in captivity or bondage from the influence of the enemy on earth. You bind demons and loose those the enemy has bound in captivity. In Luke 13:12 when Jesus set free the woman with the issue of blood, He said to her 'Woman you have been loosed (set free) from your infirmity."

Again, Jesus taught us a lesson in Matthew 12:22-29 and Luke11:14-21 about a demon possessed man who was blind and mute until Jesus healed him. In Verse 29 Jesus again illustrates this by asking the question and providing the answer. How can anyone enter a strongman's house and carry off his possessions? Unless you first bind up the strongman. Mark 3:27 indicates that we need to bind the works of the enemy, that have been influencing people's lives and situations which are not of God, instead they are of Satan who is the prince of the world, the god of this age and the ruler of the kingdom of the air (John 12:31), (2 Corinthians 4:4) and (Ephesians 2:2). There is a need to demolish every argument and every pretension that sets itself up against the knowledge of God. Moreover, we have to take captive every thought, to make it obedient to Christ (2 Corinthians 10:3-5) and as a result, to loose those in captivity who are on earth. Finally, the prayers of binding and loosing are for the salvation of men's soul, healing, liberty and God's power to be demonstrated on earth. Most of the time, the strongman builds strongholds in people's life. It can be spirit of religion, spirit of avarice and greed, spirit of violence, spirit of infirmities i.e. (sickness & diseases) and spirit of addiction just to name a few. If people are not set free from the spirit of captivity and stronghold, it will continue to rule their lives. This is where you need to bind the spirit of that stronghold which enters into their life to steal, kill and destroy. Once the power of darkness is forced to flee and the strongman is bound, the Kingdom of God can then shine through, and the glory of God will be manifested in their life on earth.

PRAYER OF AGREEMENT:

There is power in unity, oneness and agreement. In Matthew 18:19-20 Jesus affirmed that, "If two of you on earth agree about anything you ask for, it will be done by my Father who is in heaven". In verse 20 where it states that where two or three people come together in my name, there I am with them. We usually apply this scripture to a church service. Of course, It can refer to this, but what Jesus really was saying here is wherever these two people are who agree, He is right there with them to make their prayer good. (Apart from sin or anything that does not please God) Anything agreed on in the will of God by two or more people in unity and singleness of heart will be answered by God. When Believers meet together with unity, oneness, singleness of heart and one mind to pray, it produces great results (Psalm 133:1-3; Acts1:14; Acts 2:4;42-47; Act 4:29-35).

PRAYER OF REPENTANCE:

Prayers of repentance are prayers that are offered after the sinner has been convicted by the Holy Spirit of God, and where the person turns from their sin to God. They can be offered by an individual, a family, a church, or a Nation. For example, in the story of Jesus in Luke 18:9-14 concerning the Pharisee's and the tax collector's prayers, the tax collector was not able to look up to heaven but beat his chest and said "God have mercy on me a sinner"; Jesus then said that this man went home justified before God. The tax collector repented and was sorrowful, asking God graciously to reveal the truth to him. Furthermore, we find that in Luke 23:40-43 the other criminal on the cross next to Jesus, repented before God by acknowledging his wrong deeds and by asking Jesus to remember him in his Kingdom. Verse 43 reports that Jesus replied by saying that "today you will be with me in paradise".

Jonah also repented to God (Jonah 2 & 3) after he had refused to preach to the people of Nineveh and Paul repented before God on his way to Damascus (Acts 9:1-19) as a result of divine intervention. The priest/ministers and the people of the land of Judah repented and fasted before God for forgiveness of their sins and to avert judgement in Joel 1, 2 and 3 after God called them to repent.

PRAYER OF VICTORY:

This is where you pray in advance, with faith of what God can do, before and after the victory that God has given us and will be given in Christ Jesus. The psalmist David in Psalm 20 declared victory ahead of his enemies and in Proverbs 2:7 it reads "The Lord holds victory in store for the righteous". In (1 Kings 18:16-45) we see how wonderfully the Lord God through Elijah put the false prophets of Baal to shame and afterwards to death, and His name was vindicated. Another example was when Joshua and the people of Israel celebrated victory by praising God before the walls of Jericho fell down, and after they had overcome and conquered (Joshua 6). We should not forget King Jehoshaphat and the people of Judah when they also prayed a prayer of victory, petition, praise and worship. They were promised victory by God through a prophetic word by Jahaziel during the time that their three hostile enemies the Moabites, Ammonites and Meunites came to make war against them (2 Chronicles 20:1-28).

Notice in these verses King Jehoshaphat and the people of Judah continue to thank God, declare victory, giving praise and worship to God. Standing on the promises of God in faith before, during and after the battle they were facing with their enemies, God gave them victory.

PRAYER OF DEDICATION:

This type of prayer is where we present and dedicate our life, family, work, nation, or church from its beginning or any new change, any new things in your life. It also happens when we commit ourselves again to God after we or a believer has backslidden or gone away from God. Furthermore, when we had side-tracked or gone astray from Jesus, we can also rededicate our lives to the Lord in order to restore us again to fellowship with Himself. We can also present a child, a family, a church, a building, or other things to the Lord for dedication. In Luke 2:21-35 Jesus Christ was presented to the Lord by Joseph and Mary in Jerusalem. Solomon dedicated the temple of the Lord he built and the people of Israel to the Lord in 1Kings 8:22-66 and 2 Chronicles 6:12-42; 7:1-10. Our view as Christians, is to present everything to the Lord through prayer because He first gave all things to us and He is in charge of our life (1 Chronicles 29:14).

PRAYER OF COMMITMENT:

When the wind of adversity blow, we can do exactly as the word of God says, we do not have to fret or worry; we can cast our burdens on the Lord. Paul talked about this kind of prayer when he said, "Casting all your care upon him; for he care for you" (1 Peter 5:7) Casting the whole of your care, all anxieties, all your worries, all your concern, once and for all on him, God cares for you affectionately, and cares about watchfully. How wonderful that we can cast our cares upon the Lord in prayer!

It is not enough to know that God understand and is concerned. We must do what He said to do if we want to be delivered from our problem. A Scripture in the Psalms may help us see more clearly what Peter is talking about here: Commit your way to the Lord; trust also in him; and he will do it. (Psalms 37:5) Commit, cast, roll your burden on the Lord. He is not going to take away from you. Some request, "Pray that the Lord will lighten this Load; He is not going to do that. He doesn't want to just lighten your load; He wants to carry it all. But there is a vital part that we must play in this. It is a prayer of commitment. God does not want us to be anxious about anything; but in everything by prayer and petition with thanksgiving, we should present our request to God. (Philippians 4:6).

PRAYER OF SURRENDER:

Let's look at a prayer of surrender, in Apostle Paul's case, in Acts 9 When Paul met Christ on the Damascus Road he prayed, "Lord, what will you like me to do?" (Acts 9:6) That's like signing your name on a blank cheque and saying "Here I am Lord, do with me as You please. I hope I like what You choose, even if I don't, I will do it anyway; Your will be done in my life, not mine." You are deciding to voluntarily follow God rather than trying to get Him to follow you. As a result, He will do His work and put things in action, His own desires and purposes that need to be done in you and through you, so that His glory and power might be seen in you and through you. Example of Jesus in Luke 22: 41-42 when He was in the Garden of

Gethsemane offering prayers to God prior to His crucifixion. He surrendered His life to His Heavenly Father's Verse 42 paraphrased 'Father if you are willing, take this cup from me, yet not my will, but yours be done'. We can align our will to His will if we delight ourselves in Him (Psalm 37:2).

PRAYING SCRIPTURES/WORD OF GOD:

These are prayers whereby you take the written word of God in its logo (the written word of God) and use it to pray the word of God back to God and to situations and crisis. During this time as we speak and pray the scriptures, we come into agreement and align our faith with God's will and truth for our lives and then His power is released in our prayers. Hebrew 4:12 says that God's word is alive and powerful, sharper than a two-edged sword.

Using God's promises and His words by faith, what he has stated in his written word over situations, our family, church, city and nation will come to pass. Because he looks upon his words to fulfil them. (Jeremiah 1:12) Praying the word of God is also when you have memorised, meditated on God's word in your heart and you use it to pray into your situations.

PROPHETIC PRAYER:

Prophetic prayers are prayers which declare God's prophetic words, promises, instructions, comfort and edification to bring fulfilment over your life, church, family and our circumstances. These prophetic prayers always come to pass. Having faith in the words we speak; it will surely come to pass.

PREVAILING PRAYER:

All prayers are powerful. However prevailing prayers are prayers that are particularly effective and powerful. To have an idea of prevailing prayers let us look at Elijah and what prayers can do.

In 1 Kings 17:1, it was because Elijah knew how to stand before the Lord in prayer, in his secret place, that he was able to stand before King Ahab. It was his prayers in private that made him so powerful and gave him boldness in public. It was also the intensive preparation in prayer, connecting himself with God that made him to declare the prophetic word to King Ahab that "As the Lord, the God of Israel lives, before whom I stand, there shall be neither dew nor rain for three and a half years, except by my word". Let's look at prevailing prayers by the disciples in Acts 4:22, 31by which the effective prayers released by the disciples through the power of the Holy Spirit, made them bold and courageous to speak the word of the Lord and preach the word. The Lord answered them, and they were filled with the Holy Spirit and spoke the word of God boldly. The Lord performed various healing and miraculous signs through them. Also, in Acts 12:5-11 when Peter was kept in prison, the church was constantly praying to God for him and there was a miraculous intervention of him being freed! Prevailing prayers empower us to be bold and produces powerful results of salvation, healing and deliverance.

TRAVAILING AND GROANING PRAYERS:

Travailing prayers is a manifestation of the grief that is in God's heart. They are also a cry in the Spirit which can take several manifestations. Before we continue, let's see what Jesus told his disciples. He had told them that they would not see him "no more and then, after a while they would see him". In John 16:20-22 it states that "Verily, verily, I say unto you that you shall weep and lament, but the world shall rejoice, and you shall be sorrowful, but your sorrow shall be turned into joy". Verse 21 says a woman when she is giving birth has sorrow because her hour has come: but as soon as she has delivered the child, she remembers no more anguish because of her joy that a man is born into the world (John 16:22). You now therefore have sorrow: but I will see you again, and your heart shall rejoice and your joy no man can take away from you.

This is parallel to when it comes to travailing prayers to God. Perhaps we can understand it better when we realise that the Holy Spirit lives within us. Most Christians have experienced this without even realising that it is the work of the Holy Spirit. After conversion sometimes, they wept and cried, and grieved over their sins. Then they later develop a burden for the salvation and deliverance of others, and they cried over them also. This is known as travailing prayer. When we have a burden for others and things that we want to happen, we become sorrowful over their sins or in need of change, it is usually the Holy Spirit crying through us over their situation when we put that in pray until we see the outcome.

51

There is another cry which is of the flesh in relation with self-pity. Fleshly crying is always concerned about self. 2 Corinthians 7:10 states that for Godly sorrow brings repentance towards salvation and leaves no regret. For the sorrow of the world brings death. When you cry in self-pity it brings depression and fear, however crying in the Spirit brings life and joy after it has finished. (As a woman cries to bring forth a child when in labour, yet she is rejoicing as soon as the child is born). In a nutshell, travailing prayers happen when we weep and cry over something that the Holy Spirit is grieved about.

Sometimes the spirit of travailing does not manifest with visible tears of crying, but it occurs deep within us with groaning that words cannot express. It's possible to birth something in the Spirit as in Isaiah 66:8b 'As soon as Zion travailed, she brought forth her children'.

PERSISTENCE PRAYER:

Jesus, when teaching his disciples on Prayer in Luke 11:5-13, said to them that suppose one of you has a good friend, who he goes to at midnight and says, friend, lend me three loaves of bread because a friend of mine on a journey has come to me, and I have nothing to set before him. Then the one inside answers, 'Don't bother me. The door is already locked, and my children are with me in bed, I cannot get up and give you anything', I tell you, said Jesus though he will not get up and give the man the bread because he is a friend, yet because of the man's boldness (in other words because of the man persistence or pressing request) he will get up and give him as much as he needs. So, Jesus reaffirmed the exact words He used in Matthew 7:7-8   Ask and it will be given to you; seek and you will find; knock and the door will be opened to you. For everyone who ask receives, he who seeks finds and to him who knocks, the door will be opened. In this story Jesus told his disciples, we can see how diligent the man was, waking up during midnight to fend for a friend, we notice his persistence in what he needs, he was also relentless, not giving up.

In Luke 18:1-8 Jesus before telling his disciples the parable of the persistent widow, he told them that men always ought to pray and **not give up.** Jesus tells the parable of the persistent widow who kept going to the judge over and over again in order to get justice. Our Lord then declared "And will not God bring about justice to His chosen ones, who cry to him **day and night?"** Will he keep putting them off? I tell you; He will see that they get justice quickly. The Lord summed up this parable by saying that when the Son of man comes, will He find faith on earth? Will God find you still faithful or will you have given up? There are 3 important reasons why we should offer persistent prayers. There is something more important to God than God answering your prayer. God will answer your prayers at His own time and will. We have to do continuous asking, seeking and knocking and not just a single request. He can expect to answer not because of the techniques we use but because of Who is being addressed. He gave us His word of assurance and promised in Matthew 7:7-12 "Ask and it will be given to you, seek and you will find, knock and the door will be opened to you. Jesus compares our earthly father with our heavenly Father. "If our earthly father, even though evil can gave good gifts to his children, how much more will our Father in heaven give good gifts to those who ask Him"?

1. **Firstly,** God wants to keep you in His presence in order to have a relationship with you. A definite long-term relationship not a short term one. God wants a relationship, but you want things. David prayed in the morning, at noon and in the evening (Psalm 55:16-17), because he wanted to be always in His (God's) presence (Psalm 34:1).

2. **Secondly,** persistent prayer helps you to define and redefine your prayers. Sometimes we do pray amiss to consume our own lusts. God wants us to change the direction of our prayers, from self-centered prayer to God-centered prayer.

3. **Thirdly,** persistent prayer breaks the barriers of doubt and weariness. God has put you on the level of refreshing and restoration within your soul. We have two dimensions of biblical faith.

    a. Faith for eternity.
    b. Faith for today.

Faith for eternity is when a person trusts Christ's death for the payment of his or her sins and eternal salvation. This miracle takes place by the power of the Holy Spirit's work in his or her heart.

Faith for today, Hebrews 11:1 Faith is the substance of things hoped for, the evidence of things not seen. Faith is now and is an act to believe God and to put things in action. James 2:26b tells us (paraphrase) faith without works is dead. We need to believe God and to walk daily with God by faith not by sight (2 Corinthians 5:7). God has woven persistent prayer into our faith. God arranges things in a way so that our faith for today gets tested. Sometimes we have to wait for him for some specific prayers to be answered. Sometimes He allows challenges in our life that don't seem to make sense to us. God can say **yes, no, not now or wait** with regards to our prayers. He is a Sovereign God and He does what pleases him and He does it according to his will.

4. **Fourthly,** persistent prayers build in us Godly character and when we develop persistence, we become mature and complete in Christ Jesus lacking nothing.

Persistent prayers build in us Godly character James 1:4 "Let patience have her perfect work, that you may be fully mature and complete, lacking nothing."

We ask ourselves why God has not answered my prayers yet. Maybe He has answered it differently than what you expected; maybe He is waiting for you to continue praying until the ultimate answer is given. Sometimes He wants you to wait for the right season or time. This is one of the most precious insights concerning persistent prayer. Jesus shows us in his word that men should always pray and **not give up** (Luke18:1).

LOUD PRAYERS:

Our God is verbal, and He listens to us, so we should be verbal and listen to him. When we talk out loud, it reminds us that the person we are talking to is near' when we pray out loud, we remember that God is right here with us and He is listening, He cares and will act. The true God is profound and essentially verbal not only silent. God said, let there be light and it was so. He spoke. In the beginning was the word and the word become flesh and dwelt among us. So, we listen to him, we take time to hear his words full of grace and truth.

In the Psalms, relationship with God happens loud, more than 95 percent of the Psalms express audible words.

There is a place and time for loud prayers. If we follow Jesus praying on the Mount of Olives before his time of crucifixion and death, in Luke 22:44, it is written "And being in anguish, He (Jesus) prayed more earnestly, and his sweat was like drops of blood falling to the ground". When Jesus was about to die on the cross, he called out with a **loud voice to his Father** stating' Father, unto your hands I commit my spirit. (Luke 23:46). We can also confirm in Hebrews 5:6 that "During the days of Jesus's life on earth, he offered up prayers and petitions with **loud cries** and tears to the One who could save him from death". This type of prayer happens when you are desperate for something from God to sustain your life.

THE SECRET PLACE OF PRAYER

SILENT PRAYERS:

This happens when prayers are said silently to God, for example during Hannah's prayers to God in 1 Samuel 1:13. Hannah was praying in her heart and her lips were moving but **her voice was not heard**. We can follow this example of Hannah by praying from within our heart to God silently. This form of prayer is where you reverence, worship the Lord, commune with Him and ponder over the words which have been used in the worship songs in your heart to God. God desires us to worship him in spirit and in truth (John 4:24). He also urges us in 1Chronicles 16:29 to worship him in the beauty of holiness. Psalm 96:9 also confirms that we have to worship the Lord in the splendour of his holiness. Also, silent prayers can take the form of meditating on the word of God in your heart (Psalm 1:2), (Psalm 5:1), (Joshua 1:8) as the word of God instruct us.

IMPRECATION/JUDGEMENTAL OR CURSE PRAYERS:

These can be defined as praying for God to vindicate the righteous from their enemies. It also goes beyond that to the extent that you may invoke evil and curses on your enemies. King David in the Book of Psalms is sometimes associated with imprecatory prayers and verses. In Psalm 55:9-15 David invokes curse and death to his enemies; in Psalms 69:28 David wants his enemies to be blotted out in the book of the living, and not be written with the righteous. Psalms 109:8 Psalms 35:6

also demonstrates imprecation prayers, to name but a few.

However, in the New Testament, which is the new covenant, Jesus words in Matthew (5:43-44) states that, "you have heard that it was said, love your neighbour and hate your enemies, but I tell you to love your enemies and pray for those who persecute you." This commandment or instruction from Jesus supersedes all previous imprecatory prayers. We do this in order to become sons and daughters of our Father in Heaven. We are told, in Romans 12:19-21 we should not avenge ourselves, but to leave room for God's wrath and vengeance, it is written vengeance belong to the Lord, He will repay. Paraphrasing Romans12:20-21- we are to feed our enemies if they are hungry, give them drink if they are thirsty, and we should not be overcome by evil, but overcome evil with good. It will do us well to note we are in the New Covenant!

CHAPTER 5

INSTRUCTIONS ABOUT PRAYER

WHAT IS PRAYER?

Prayer is a communication process that allows us to talk to and with God and is the intercourse of the soul with God. Not in contemplation or meditation (as with the eastern incantations) but in direct address to God. Prayer can be oral, mental, occasional, constant, or formal. It is also the breath of God and the master key that unlocks heaven and locks the gates of hell. Real prayer is expressing our sincere devotion to our heavenly father, inviting us to talk to Him as He talks to us.

Communication is probably one of the most important activities in life. There are different kinds of communication.

In the words of Myles Munroe's definition of prayer, he said: "Prayer is man giving God permission to interfere in the affairs of men on earth".

In Luke 18:1-8 the Lord commissions us that, we should always pray and not to give up. Verse 7 says: "Will not God bring justice for His chosen ones, who cry to Him day and night?"

Will He keep putting them off?

The Lord Jesus taught us the importance of prayer. Man is spirit, have a soul and live in a body (Genesis 2:7; 1st Thessalonians 5:23), and his major needs are essentially spiritual. This is why man always craves for that spiritual contact or connection with God, who is described in Hebrews 12:9 as the Father of our spirits.

What a blessing it is to know that you can communicate directly with your heavenly Father and He hears us (Matt 6:9; Romans 5:2; Hebrew 4:16); that you can have His total attention through prayer: "For the eyes of the Lord are over the righteous, and His ears are open unto their prayers, but the face of the Lord is against them that do evil'(1 Peter 3:12). However, Isaiah 59:1 tell us that 'Surely the arm of the Lord is not too short to save, nor His ear too dull to hear. But our iniquities have separated us from God'.

WHO CAN PRAY?

Anyone can pray, but those who have relationship with God, walking in faith and obedience to His Will, can expect to receive answers to their prayers.

Contact with God begins when we sincerely repent of our sins and we receive Jesus Christ as our personal Saviour and Lord (John 3:16; John 1:12; John 14:6; Romans 10:9-10 and 1 John 1:9).

WHY ARE WE TO PRAY?

God's word commands us to pray (Luke 18:1; Matthew 26:41; Acts 6:4; Mark 14:38; Philippians 4:6; Colossians 4:2 and I Timothy 2:1, 2).

We pray to have fellowship with God, receive spiritual nurture through His word, and also to get direction and strength to live victorious lives, to receive strength, maintain confidence and boldness for a vital witness for Christ and furthermore, to destroy the works of the devil.

Praying is discovering God's revealed purpose in Scripture, and then praying for the outworking of that purpose.

We pray to release God's great power to change the course of nature, people and nations.

TO WHOM DO WE PRAY?

We pray to the Father in the name of the Lord Jesus Christ through the power and ministry of the Holy Spirit. When we pray to the Father, our prayers are accepted by Jesus Christ and interpreted to God the Father by the Holy Spirit (Romans 8: 26, 27, 34).

WHEN SHOULD WE PRAY?

God's word commands us to "pray continually" as in 1 Thessalonians 5:17. We can be in prayer throughout the day. We can choose to pray in the morning, afternoon or evening as the Spirit of God leads us and how we schedule our day.

We can follow some typical examples of David (a man of prayer) in the book of Psalms (Psalm 55:16-17) which says "I call to God and the Lord saved me. Evening, morning and noon I cry in distress, and He hears my voice". Psalm 88:13 states that "I cry for help. O Lord, in the morning my prayers come before you." David's prayer also in Psalm 141:2 expresses that his prayer be set before God like incense and may his lifting up of his hands be like the evening sacrifice. Also, like Daniel who prayed, giving thanks to his God on his knees three times a day (Daniel 6:9-10), we can be expressing and demonstrating our devotion to God as we go about our daily tasks.

HOW THEN DO WE PRAY?

Sometimes we pray like Hannah, moving our lip and praying silently. Sometimes like Daniel, who bowed his knees three times in a day. Sometimes with deep sighs like Jesus in Mark 7:34 when He prayed for the healing of a deaf and mute man, or it could be loud as Jesus did in Luke 22:43 and Hebrews 5:7. We could offer prayers as long as Solomon's at the dedication of the temple (II Chronicles 6).

Be led by the Spirit of God as to how you ought to pray. Paul reiterated in Ephesians 6:18 that we have to pray in the Spirit on all occasions, with all kinds of prayers and requests.

HOW DO I DISPOSITION MYSELF WHEN I AM PRAYING?

It is not always necessary to be on our knees, fold both hands or be in a quiet room to pray. You can do that if you wish (Luke 22:41 and Mathew 6:6). God wants us to be in touch with Him in prayer constantly wherever we are. Let us see some examples in the bible. King Solomon in 1Kings 8:22 spread his hands towards heaven. Paul encourages us in 1Timothy 2:8 that "he (Paul) wants all men everywhere to lift up holy hands in prayer, without anger or disputing".

In Luke 22:41 Jesus knelt down for prayers. In Acts 20:36 Paul knelt down and prayed for all his disciples before departing by ship on his way to Jerusalem.

King Solomon knelt down and spread his hands to heaven to pray. We can pray while sitting down or standing (1 Samuel 1:26). 2 Chronicles 6:13).

Ezekiel lay down on his left side and on his right side (Ezekiel 4:1-9) and in 1 Kings 18:42b, Elijah bent down to the ground, bowing and putting his face between his knees to pray.

In 2 Chronicles 20:5 Jehoshaphat stood up to pray to the Lord for deliverance and victory from his enemies.

You can also pray in your car, whilst washing the dishes, walking down the street, walking in the park ... you can also find a quiet place to pray as Jesus did.

The most important thing is not the disposition of the body but the condition of the soul, if the heart is attuned to God, one can pray in any posture or place imaginable as led by the Holy Spirit.

WHO TO PRAY WITH?

We can pray as an individual, with our spouse, our child/children, with a prayer partner, with our spiritual mentor, work colleague, in a group or in a church congregation.

DOES PRAYER REALLY CHANGE THINGS?

Though our prayers do not change God's mind, He ordains prayer as a means to accomplish His will. We can be confident that prayer does change things, including our hearts and to implement things according to His purpose and will. Throughout the bible records, we have noticed that God change things and situations through the prayers of faithful men and women.

WHAT SHOULD WE INCLUDE IN OUR PRAYERS?

Although prayer cannot be reduced to a formula, certain basic elements should be included in our communication with God. Adoration, Confession, Thanksgiving, and Supplication (ACTS) as Jesus taught us in Matthew 6:9-14.

A - Adoration

To adore God is to worship Him for who He is, His nature, characteristics and to praise Him for what He has done, to honour and exalt Him in our heart and mind and with our lips.

C - Confession

Before or during our time of prayer, we begin with adoration. The Holy Spirit then has the opportunity to reveal any sin in our life that needs to be confessed and, as a result, will be willing to accept our sincere confessions to God.

T - Thanksgiving

We have to show an attitude of thanksgiving and gratitude to God, for what he has done and the benefits we enjoy because we belong to Him, He enables us to recognise that he controls all things, not we ourselves - not just the blessings but our problems and adversities as well. As we approach God with a thankful heart, He recognise that we are grateful for His grace and blessings on our life.

S - Supplication

Supplication is generally a request by the person praying to the one they are praying to. It includes a petition for our own needs and for the needs of others. Pray that your inner person may be renewed, be always sensitive to and be empowered by the Holy Spirit. Supplication entails praying for others - your spouse, your children, your parents, neighbours and friends, your workplaces, your churches, your nation and those in authority over you. Pray for the salvation of souls, for a daily opportunity to introduce others to Christ and to the ministry of the Holy Spirit and for the fulfilment of the Great Commission.

As a suggestion, you can also plan your prayer schedule as some Christians do as led by the Holy Spirit. For example:

Monday: Pray for family and friends.

Tuesday: Workplace and colleagues.

Wednesday: Church leaders and members.

Thursday: Pray for yourself.

Friday: Your nation including your leaders and their cities.

Saturday: For lost souls in your neighbourhood.

Sunday: Your pastor and your church leaders.

CHAPTER 6

PRAYERS IN THE OLD TESTAMENT

In patriarchal times, prayer was often described as calling on the name of the Lord. Men started to call on the name of the Lord in Genesis 4:26, after Seth's son Enosh who is Adam's grandson, was born.

Prayer started from this generation of Adam after the fall of mankind. In Genesis 12: 8, Abram was called to go towards the hills, east of Bethel, and pitch his tent with Bethel on the west and Ai on the east. There he built an altar to the Lord and called on the name of the Lord in worship and prayed in regard to the promise and the journey he was about to undertake.

We see also from Genesis 13:3-4 that on his return, Abram again called on the name of the Lord when he got to the same place between Bethel and Ai where he had originally pitched his tent and built an altar. Prayers transcend through the generations of Israel. In Deuteronomy 4:7, The Lord God commanded and assured the people of Israel that they have a great God (Him), and He is near to them whenever and wherever they pray to Him.

This assured the people of Israel to trust God more and offer prayers to Him. It also assures us of the closeness of our God when we pray. There are many prophets and Kings in the Old Testament that had the testimony of the power of prayer because they prayed and then prevailed. Priests, soldiers, prophets, married women, Queens, reformers and widows had difficulties and challengers, but they overcame them by the power of prayer. The prayers of these men and women of God were supernatural, miraculous and wondrous because God worked on their behalf through their prayers.

Let us see some individuals in the Old Testament who prayed to God who is in heaven, and this was accompanied by supernatural answers on the earth. These men and women were connected to God through prayers, and their prayers are recorded for us to understand what we can do and that God hears our prayers!

ABRAHAM'S PRAYER: A MAN OF PRAYER: GENESIS 18:16-33

In the book of Genesis, Abraham (friend of God) was the first notable person whose text was recorded in the Torah and Hebrew with a prayer of intercession. Abraham pleads with

God not to destroy the people of Sodom where his nephew Lot resided.

Abraham listened to God. He was willing to set out for whatever God commanded and to do what God willed. By this listening and his readiness to make a new start, he is a model of our prayers. His plea for Sodom is the first great intercessory prayer in the history of God's People.

As God's revelations became fuller and more perfect, Abraham's prayerful life increased, and it was at one of these spiritual eras that Abraham fell on his face and talked with God. What a remarkable story of Abraham standing before God, repeating his intercessions for the wicked city of Sodom, the home of his nephew Lot, doomed by God's decision to destroy it. Sodom's fate was stayed a while by Abraham praying and was almost entirely relieved by the humility and insistence of the praying of this man who believed strongly in prayer and who knew how to pray. No other recourse was open to Abraham to save Sodom but prayer. Perhaps the failure to ultimately rescue Sodom from her doomed destruction was due to Abraham's optimistic view of the spiritual condition of things in that city. It might be possible who knows, that if Abraham had entreated God one more time, and asked Him to spare the city if even one righteous man was found there, God might have heeded Abraham's request for His (God's) sake.

Another instance in the life of Abraham as showing he was a man of prayer and had power with God, was when Abraham had journeyed to and was staying at Gerar. Fearing that Abimelech might kill him and appropriate Sarah his wife to that king's own lustful uses, he deceived Abimelech by claiming that Sarah was his sister. God appeared too Abimelech in a dream and warned Abimelech not to touch Sarah telling him that she was the wife of Abraham not his sister. Then God said to Abimelech 'Now restore therefore the man his wife, for he is a prophet, and he shall pray for you, and you shall live'. So the conclusion of the matter was that Abraham prayed to God and God healed Abimelech, his wife and maidservants and they were able to bear children.

It was Abraham's rule to stand before the Lord in prayer. His life was surcharged with prayer and Abraham's disposition was sanctified by prayer. Wherever he halted in his pilgrimage, prayer was an inseparable accompaniment. Side by side with the altar of sacrifice was the altar of prayer. He got up early in the morning to the place where he stood before the Lord in Prayer. Let us emulate how Abraham walked with God in prayer.

MOSES' PRAYER:

Moses walked and communicated with God like no other person recorded in the Old Testament. God, together with Moses, experienced continual complaints from the people of

Israel. It started over the lack of water, and it continued throughout the rest of Moses' life. In spite of Moses' constant struggles, he endured the course of his calling from God and did not give up. By his leadership the Red Sea was divided miraculously by God for the people of Israel to cross. Moses called out and God answered.

In Exodus 15:25, Moses cried unto the Lord and the Lord showed him a piece of wood, which, when he had thrown it in the water, the water was made sweet. God made for them a statute and an ordinance, and He commissioned them that if they listen to and obey His commands, He will prove and fulfil His promise to them, especially healing and deliverance. This shows us that in desperation, we should not complain or give up but pray, listen and trust in our God. Moses prayed and God answered again in Exodus 17:4-6. In Numbers 11, Moses prayed to the Lord and the Lord dried up the fire which consumed the Israelites who had complained about their hardship. In Numbers 12:13-14, Moses cried out to the Lord to heal his sister Miriam after the Lord had inflicted leprosy on her for rebelling against Moses. Again, the Lord God answered. Moses prayed on behalf of the people of Israel so that God would not destroy them, standing before God in the breach, to turn away His (God's) wrath.

JEHOSHAPHAT'S PRAYER:

In 2 Chronicles 20, we read of the testimony of Jehoshaphat.

When three nations threatened them and were about to make war against him and his nation, it was recorded that Jehoshaphat, King of Judah in Jerusalem, was not in discomfort neither did he complain. Instead, he decided to enquire of the Lord (prayed to the Lord God) and proclaim a fast with the people of Judah who came together to seek (to pray) for help from the Lord. Verse 5 records that Jehoshaphat stood up in the congregation of Judah and Jerusalem in the temple of the Lord in front of the new courtyard and prayed to the Lord with the help of the people of Judah.

The Spirit of the Lord came upon Jahaziel, son of Zechariah, to say to King Jehoshaphat and the people of Judah and Jerusalem that they should not be afraid or discouraged because of the vast army. For the battle was not theirs, but God's.
The Lord showed them the strategy to use, and the Lord was with them throughout the battle.

Jehoshaphat bowed his face to worship before the Lord and sang praises to the Lord (II Chronicles 20:18-27). Bible records show that the vast army from the three nations, who wanted to attack Judah and Jerusalem started fighting and attacking each other in their own camp until all of them were destroyed.

When the men of Judah came to the battlefield expecting to find a vast army, they only found dead bodies lying on the ground and no one had escaped so Jehoshaphat and his men carried everything (booty) that belonged to the enemy.

The load was so much that it took three days for them to collect. On the following day, they praised and celebrated the Lord for victory over their enemies. God is set to normalise any unpleasant circumstances in times of trouble when we call upon Him in faith.

We can learn a lesson here and witness that when the people of God fast, pray, worship and praise the Lord in times of conflict, or when challenged in ugly situations or difficult situations, whether it is spiritual or physical, the Lord God will fight the battle for them. He will give them victory through our spiritual weapons and by the power of God.

This is how God would confuse and destroy the powers of darkness if we are prepared to pray, worship, fast, humble ourselves and praise Him.

JABEZ'S PRAYER:

The scripture says in 1 Chronicles 4:9-10 that Jabez was more honourable (upright, commanded high respect) than his brothers. His mother had named him Jabez saying that she gave birth to him in pain. Jabez prayed a simple and straight forward prayer. **He cried to the Lord God** of Israel from his heart, a sincere and a heartfelt prayer. He prayed that God should bless him and enlarge his territory! That God's hand should be with him and keep him from harm so that he will be free from pain; and God granted his request. We notice that Jabez prayed with a sincere heart. He was honest, prayed in faith, and was specific to God about his request and it was granted. We need to come to God with an honest and sincere heart (genuine repentance/no hidden sin) and full of faith to receive from God.

SOLOMON'S PRAYER:

After the Lord appeared to King Solomon during the night in a dream, he requested from King Solomon to ask for whatever he wanted God to give him. In 1 Kings 3:5 the Bible records that Solomon prayed asking God since he had made him servant and King over this great people, too numerous to count, that God should give him a discerning heart to govern God's people and to distinguish between right and wrong (verses 6-15). The Lord was pleased with Solomon for asking for wisdom and understanding to govern God's people and God granted his request. He furthermore added favour, wealth, honour and long life to King Solomon.

The Lord requires us to ask Him for things that please Him and things that favour and advance His kingdom's work and as a result, He can add all things to us. For example, His righteousness, wisdom, understanding and fulfilling His Great Commission as our priority.

When Solomon was dedicating the Lord's Temple in 1 Kings 8:22-66, we learn that King Solomon stood before the altar of the Lord in front of the whole assembly of Israel. He spread out his hands towards heaven as he prayed and dedicated the

Temple of the Lord. Solomon also gave thanksgiving and offered supplications for the people of Israel. This also shows us that, today, God fearing Kings and leaders of a nation have the mandate to pray for their nations and God will hear and answer them. This is evident in this chapter up until verse 66. Solomon offered different kinds of prayers to God, which will be discussed in the forthcoming chapter.

HANNAH'S PRAYER:

In 1Samuel1:1-20 Hannah was very sorrowful and had a bitter soul because the Lord had shut up her womb and she was being provoked by her rival Peninnah (1 Samuel 1:10). As she was in bitterness of soul, she prayed to the Lord and wept. Hannah made a vow to the Lord. She prayed that the Lord should look at her affliction, remember and not forget her, God give her a male child who she would then give to the Lord all the days of his life.

(Verse 12) Hannah continued to pray before the Lord, and Eli observed her mouth. (Verse 13) Hannah prayed in her heart, only her lips moved, but her voice was not heard.

Verse 1:19b shows us that Elkanah knew Hannah his wife and the Lord remembered her and she conceived. Thereafter, when the time was come that Hannah conceived, she bared a son and she called him Samuel because I have asked him of the Lord.

This shows us that the Lord answers when we pray in our affliction, bitterness of soul, desperation or when we are downcast, to fulfil His and our heart's desires (Psalm 37:4).

ELIJAH'S PRAYER:

Elijah's prayers are effective and powerful. To have an idea of Elijah's prayers let us look at some of the healing, restoration and miracles he brought about and what prayers can do.

In 1st Kings 17:1, it was because Elijah knew how to stand before the Lord in prayer that he was able to stand before King Ahab. In 1st Kings 17, it was his prayers in private that made him powerful in public before the King. It was also his intensive prayers and connecting with God that made him to declare to King Ahab that "As the Lord, the God of Israel lives, before whom I stand, there shall be neither dew nor rain these years, except by my word".

Elijah continued to pray in 1st Kings 18:42b elaborating the request as he went up to the top of Mount Carmel, bowed himself down on the earth and put his face between his knees. Elijah prayed intensively and reliantly and, as a result, (verse 45) the heavens grew black with clouds and wind, and there was a great rain. This was after they had experienced three years of severe drought and famine in the land of Samaria.

On another occasion, the prophet Elijah prayed for the widow of Zarephath's dead son (1 Kings 17:17-24). He took him to the upper room where he stretched himself out on the dead boy three times and prayed to the Lord God for the boy's life to return to him. The Lord heard Elijah's cry and the boy's life returned to him and he lived. The Lord restores life and works miracles through men of God and Christians who live a sincere, righteous and prayerful life.

In the next chapter (1Kings 18: 19-39) we notice that there was a challenge between the prophet Elijah and the prophets of Baal. These people wanted to prove who the real and living God was. Either the God that Elijah serves or their god, over a sacrifice of a bull on wood and stone without setting fire to it. The God who answers by fire would be God (Verse 25-26). The prophets of Baal called on the name of their Baal from morning to noon but there was no response, and no one answered. Their sacrifice did not catch fire.

However, in verses 36-39, Prophet Elijah prayed to the Living God, the God of Abraham, Isaac and Israel, to answer him, so that the people may know that the Lord is God. Then the fire of the Lord fell and consumed his sacrifice which was drenched with four large jars of water. God answered by causing fire to burn up the sacrifice, the wood, stones, the soil and it also licked up the water in the trench. When all the people saw this miraculous act of God and that He does answer prayer, they fell prostrate and cried: "The Lord - He is God. The Lord - He is God. This challenge shows us how God, who Christians worship, is a living God and is ready to answer our prayers so as to show Himself as God when we pray. Prayer works and is relevant in our lives and that of others.

ELISHA'S PRAYER:

In 2 Kings 6:8-17, the King of Syria warred against Israel and took counsel with his servants. The heart of the King was troubled, and he wanted to know which of his aides was for the King of Israel, as all his war plans against Israel seemed to be known to the King of Israel.

One of the King's servants informed him that Elisha the prophet had been telling the King of Israel the words that the King of Syria had been saying in his bedchamber (bedroom). He did send his army by night to encompass the city of Dothan in Israel, because he had been told Elisha lived there.

When the servant of Elisha woke up in the morning and saw the vast army, he was afraid and asked Elisha his master "What shall we do?" (2 Kings 6:15-16) Elisha replied back and encouraged him: "Fear not, for they that be with us are more than they that be with them."

(Verse 17) records that Elisha prayed, and said, "I pray to you Lord, open his eyes that he may see". And the Lord opened the eyes of the young man; (the servant) and he saw that the mountain was full of horses and chariots of fire around Elisha.

Elisha again prayed to the Lord to strike the Syrian army with blindness and, according to the word of Elisha, the Lord did strike them with blindness. Elisha later directed them to the wrong city in Samaria. Elisha prayed again to the Lord to open these men's eyes to see. Then the Lord opened their eyes to see that they were captive in Samaria. Great food and drink was set before them for a while, and he ordered to send them back later to their master in Syria. So, the bands of Syria did not come back anymore to the land of Israel (verse 20).

The Lord fights our battles for us and causes us to have victory over our enemies when we are prayerful and when we pray in difficult situations. We also need to pray so that God will open our spiritual eyes to see His supernatural work and to give us spiritual understanding.

We can also see that in 2 Kings 4:32, when Elisha was informed of the Shunammite woman's dead son, he shut the door on two of them (Elisha and the dead boy) and prayed by stretching himself on the boy. The boy's body grew warm, and Elisha walked back and forth in the room stretching again on the boy and the boy sneezed seven times, opened his eyes and became alive again.

God can restore and bring dead people to life if we believe. Pray in faith and if it is according to His divine will, He will answer.

NEHEMIAH'S PRAYERS:

In the book of Nehemiah, it was recorded that Nehemiah mourned, fasted and prayed day and night for the servants and the people of Israel. One of Nehemiah's prayers before he started rebuilding the ruined wall of Jerusalem was in Nehemiah 1:5-6 which states "O' Lord, God of heaven, the great and awesome God, who keeps his covenant of love with those who love Him and obey His commands.

Verse 6: "Let your ear be attentive and your eyes open to hear the prayer your servant is praying before you, day and night, for your servants and the people of Israel. I confess the sins that we Israelites, including myself and my father's house have committed against you". These powerful words reveal Nehemiah's steadfast belief in the power of God.

Nehemiah is able to pray with conviction because he knows that his confidence is in God. Even though he faced the impossible task of rebuilding the ruined wall of Jerusalem, (after the wall of Jerusalem and its gates had been broken and burned down, the Jewish remnants who had survived the exile, were back in the province, troubled and disgraced), Nehemiah knew that God was still on His throne. He did this before the God of heaven, . Nehemiah did confess the sins of the Israelites, including his sins and those of his father's household. He prayed for God's direction, strength and protection and prayed against any opposition in rebuilding the walls of Jerusalem. In Nehemiah Chapter4:14b, Nehemiah urged the people not to be afraid of the enemy but to earnestly remember the Lord and he encouraged them to be mindful of Him greatly. They must take from God, courage to fight (pray, call out) for their brethren, their sons, daughters, wives, and homes until the completion of the wall of Jerusalem. Church leaders who are building and restoring the house of God (God's people) are to be encouraged to pray continually for God's direction, strength and protection in times of opposition to building God's Kingdom.

HEZEKIAH'S PRAYERS:

King Hezekiah of Judah went to the temple of the Lord and prayed to the God of Heaven when Sennacherib King of Assyria, threatened and made war against Jerusalem. The Lord God saved and delivered them from the hands of their enemies (2 Kings 19:15).

God is ready to listen to God-fearing Kings and leaders who seek His face when their nations are being threatened by an enemy.

On another occasion, when the King became ill to the point of death (Isaiah 38; 2 Kings 20:1-11), King Hezekiah turned his face to the wall, prayed, pleaded his cause and wept bitterly to the Lord. The Lord God gave confirmation and instruction, through prophet Isaiah that He had heard Hezekiah's prayers and tears and would heal him. Furthermore, that He will add fifteen more years to his life. This signifies that God has compassion on people, hears their prayers and that, there is healing for Kings, leaders and everyone who seeks and prays to God, with a repented and sincere heart for their situation.

JONAH'S PRAYERS:

Jonah was sent by God to proclaim the good news to the people of Nineveh and their need to repent. When he refused, the Lord God provided a great fish to swallow Jonah and he was inside the belly of the fish for three days and three nights.
While he was in the fish, Jonah prayed to the Lord to deliver him from his distress and asked for repentance and help. The Lord heard Jonah's prayers and commanded the fish to vomit Jonah out on to dry land (Jonah 2:1-10).

We can see that Jonah repented of his initial disobedience to the Lord, and subsequently obeyed the Lord's command, which in turn led to the repentance of the people in Nineveh. The people of Nineveh fasted and prayed and even their animals did the same (Jonah 3).
The Lord was merciful to the people of Nineveh as there came about a change and revival in the land.
God is ever ready to listen and be merciful to people who have been wicked and disobedient, provided they turn to Him with a sincere, repented, remorseful heart and have faith in Him.

DAVID'S PRAYERS:

At the time that King David began his rulership of the people of Israel (1 Chronicles 17:16-27), he prayed to God for God's promises which had been given to him. In these promises, God had told David that He would make his name like the names of the greatest men on the earth and would give him victory over his enemies.

David also offered prayers of thanksgiving after he and the people of Israel had contributed generously towards the building of the Temple that the Lord God had promised his son Solomon would build (1 Chronicles 29:10-20).

The Lord requires us to offer to Him prayers of thanksgiving before He fulfils His promises and also after fulfilling them. It gives Him the pleasure to do more for His people who appreciate Him and acknowledge what He has done.

After King David premeditated the murder of Bathsheba's husband, he spent all night fasting and praying pleading to God for his adulterous related born child with Bathsheba not to die. David was also rebuked by God through the Prophet Nathan (2 Samuel 12:16). David repented of all of his sins. Psalm 51 assures us of the sincere prayer of David. This makes it clear as to why God called him a man after his own heart and a friend of God. In the Psalms we notice that anytime David is in distress or dismay, is fearful or disappointed, in need of deliverance, when defeated, in need of help or protection, he will confess, worship and pray to the living God. The entire book of Psalms, written primarily by David, contains at least seven other writers, including the sons of Korah and is full of prayers and praises.

Despite our numerous sins, when we turn away from them in sincere repentance, God is faithful to forgive us and cleanse us from all our sins (1 John 1:9).
In 2 Samuel 15:31 David also prayed, and God defeated the foolish counsel of Ahithophel when he conspired with Absalom to take David's life and the kingdom.

JEREMIAH'S PRAYERS:

The prophet Jeremiah prayed for himself and prayed also that God would pour out this wrath on nations who do not acknowledge and call upon the name of the Lord God but who instead, want to devour and destroy Israel (Jeremiah 10:23-25).

Jeremiah urged the people of Israel to arise, to cry out in the night and in the beginning of the night watch to pour out their hearts like water before the presence of the Lord. They should also lift up their hands towards Him for the life of their young children who faint of hunger at the top of every street (Lamentations 2:19). For Jeremiah, prayer was an agonising experience (Jeremiah 20:7; Jeremiah 9:1-10). Jeremiah also prayed for God to intervene in Judah (Jeremiah 14:7-9 and19-

22) when there was a drought in the land of Judah due to their pride, idolatry, rebellion, falsehood and false professing by the prophets. He also saw prayer as an intimate communion with God (Jeremiah 15:11-21) where he prayed, and God answered by giving him instructions to follow.

EZEKIEL'S PRAYERS:

Ezekiel was instructed by the Lord to intercede (putting the sin of the house of Israel upon himself and bearing their sins for the number of days that he has to lie on his side) for the people of Israel and for Jerusalem (Ezekiel 4:1-9). God instructed him by erecting a siege around Jerusalem and also for him to lie on his left side for 390 days and on the right side for 40 days for the iniquity of the house of Judah, a day for each year.

ESTHER AND MORDECAI'S PRAYERS:

In the book of Esther, Chapter 4, Esther, Mordecai and all the Jews who lived in the city of Susa fasted and prayed to God so that He would intervene and defeat the craftiness and evil plan of Haman and save the Jews from destruction. God made a way for that to happen, and the Jews were saved from destruction. In addition, honour and favour was given to Mordecai and the Jews. God is ever ready to intervene and destroy the plans of the evil one against His people when His people offer prayers and intercede. God also gives us favour before Kings and with people who are in authority when we fast and pray to Him for divine intervention.

DANIEL'S PRAYER:

Daniel was a man of prayer who possessed exceptional qualities and an excellent spirit. He prayed three times a day on his knees, in his upstairs room, with the windows open towards Jerusalem giving thanks and asking God for help, as was his practice (Daniel 6:10-11).

God also delivered and rescued Daniel from the lions' den when there was a conspiracy against him, and he was charged with praying to his Living God (Daniel 6:21).

God rescues and delivers upright, faithful, and prayerful people from injustice and from false accusation by authorities of the land.

Daniel also confessed, pleaded and interceded on behalf of the people of Israel (Chapter 9: 3, 4, 20-23).

Daniel's earnest prayers were heard and responded to immediately on the first day that he set his mind and heart to pray, concerning the things that will happen to the people of Israel and their land in the future. However, for twenty-one days, there was a resistance (for the answer to reach Daniel) by the Prince of Persia (the enemy). The archangel of the Lord (Michael) had to come and deal with this prince in the heavenly for the messenger angel to be able to get to Daniel and reveal the answer to him (Daniel 10). God gave Daniel an interpretation of a vision, understanding and insight for the things to come in the future.

There is a place of warfare in prayer. We need to earnestly and desperately resist the enemy until the answer to prayer reaches us from Heaven. In Ezekiel 22:30, God was seeking men and women who would stand in the gap, in prayer before Him and on behalf of the land, so that He would not destroy it and its inhabitants, however He found no-one.

The story of Daniel shows us that consistent, effective and fervent prayer should be observed daily for the nations, city, churches, pastors, ministers, leaders, and families to obey and walk in the ways of God, and for spiritual harvest of people to turn from their wicked ways to God.

CHAPTER 7

JESUS'S ONGOING LIFE OF PRAYER

A clear perspective of the actual life and ministry of Jesus can be realised as we follow him from one prayer meeting to the next, in the same manner that Jesus's disciples followed him from one place of prayer to another throughout Christ's earthly ministry.

In between those places of prayer, we see the power of God manifested and flowing out of Him and meeting every need, saving people from their sins, setting people free, healing the sick and providing for the people.

After the baptism of Jesus by John the Baptist and prior to his ministry, the bible says in Matthew 4:1-11 that he was led by the Spirit into the desert to be tempted by the devil.
After fasting for forty days and forty nights he was hungry. I believe that Jesus' fasting was accompanied by prayer. That is why he was able to be strengthened by the power of God and was able to use the word of God to overcome the devil's

temptations. This waiting on God by fasting and prayer helped him to prepare for his ministry.

At the beginning of Christ's ministry, we read "**Very early in the morning,** while it was still dark, Jesus got up, left the house and went off to a **solitary place** (a place of quietness, without companions) where he prayed" (Mark 1:35).

The writer Luke (Luke 6:12) reminds us that, in the days of Jesus' early ministry, he went up on the mountain side to pray and spent **all night** praying to God.

In the middle of His ministry, after hearing the bad news of John the Baptist being beheaded and before miraculously feeding the five thousand, we read in Matthew 14:13, that Jesus withdrew himself and went up to **a solitary place to pray.**

We also notice that after the feeding of the 5,000 and dismissing the disciples to the other side by using a boat, Jesus went to the **mountainside to pray alone till the evening (**Matthew 14:23). On one occasion, (Luke 9:28-29), Jesus took three of his disciples with him and went up unto the **mountain to pray.** While he was praying, the appearance of his face changed, and his clothes became as bright as a flash of lightning.

In John's gospel (John 17:1-26) we recall that, before his arrest and trial, Jesus prayed what is called The High Priestly Prayers" He looked towards heaven and **prayed for himself,**

his disciples and all believers. In part, this is the longest recorded prayer of Jesus, which is called the high priestly prayers because of His intercessory prayers for those who come to believe in Him. He prayed that God would protect them - that is us- from the power of the devil who was bound to attack. He continues to pray even today, "since He always lives to make intercession for [us]" (Hebrews 7:25).

In Luke's account in Luke 22:39-45, before Jesus was about to be betrayed and arrested in the Garden of Gethsemane, whilst he was at the Mount of Olives, it was recorded that "**he knelt down and prayed and being in anguish, he prayed more earnestly,** and his sweat was like drops of blood falling to the ground".

At the end of his earthly ministry the book of Luke tells us that Jesus went out to the Mount of Olives, as was his habit, to pray (Luke 22:39,40). Even on the cross we see **Jesus praying** (Luke 23:34, 46) "Jesus said Father' forgive them, for they do not know what they are doing". In verse 46, Jesus called out with a loud voice, "Father, into your hands I commit my spirit. As he was dying, he said, "It is finished" (John 19:30).

However, His death did not mark the end of His prayer ministry.

Apostle Paul reassures us (Romans 8:34) that Jesus the risen Christ is at the right hand of God and also making intercession for us.

It was also reconfirmed in Romans 8:34a and Hebrews 7:25 that Jesus is in heaven today and is interceding for us. He is able to completely save those who come to God through him because he ever lives to make intercession for us. Jesus' continuing ministry **in heaven is prayer.** Be assured you are being prayed for today by your High Priest and intercessor, Jesus Christ.

BE A DISCIPLE OF JESUS

Apart from winning souls for the kingdom of God and following the Great Commission, we need prayers and the empowerment of the Holy Spirit for the work of God.

Jesus has given us the Holy Spirit to help us when we pray (Romans 8:26, 27).

First the Holy Spirit births within us the DESIRE to pray. Second, as we obey, this desire matures within us and moves us into a place of holy DISCIPLINE before the Lord. Jesus' life was a disciplined life of prayer, and the power of God flows out of him every time after prayers. If we want to see the power of God move in our lives, **there must be a continuous renewal of our relationship with God through a consistent, daily prayer life.**

After we discipline ourselves to be consistent in prayer, this consistent prayer moves us to the third level which is to experience a DELIGHT in praying. Therefore, the process starts off by having a desire, then discipline and finally to delight in prayer. Here, we delight to pray according to His will and to do His will. We then rejoice in His presence, His power, His protection and His provision. Psalm 37:4 states, as we delight ourselves in the Lord, He gives us the desires of our heart. These are His desires. His desires become our desires!

CHAPTER 8

JESUS'S MODEL OF PRAYER – A.C.T.S

Given that prayer is so important and central to what we are as human beings it was natural for Jesus's followers to ask him to teach them how to pray.

In Matthew Chapter 6.5-9 and in a shorter version in Luke 11:1-4, Jesus taught his disciples, and we being his followers (disciples), how to pray. Verses 5 to 13 of Matthew Chapter 6, Jesus taught and showed us a typical model of prayer. Jesus said, when we pray we should go into our room, close the door and pray to our Father, who is unseen and then our Father, who sees what is done in secret, will reward us. Jesus later shows us the pattern to pray in verse 9 to 13. He said. "This is how you should pray."

Step One - *Our Father who art in Heaven, Hallowed be thy name.* This marks the beginning of the first prayer topic. Jesus teaches us how to pray and appropriate his promises. Here you enter the presence of God, acknowledge and adore him as the Father, who He is. You can use God's covenant names composed with Jehovah in the Old Testament: example: Jehovah **Tsidekenu**: our righteousness - Jeremiah. 23:6, **Eloheenu:** Our God - Psalm 99:5,8,9, **El-Shaddai:** our sufficiency -Genesis 22:17, **Shammah**: God is present - Ezekiel 48:35, **Saboath:** Lord of Hosts - 1Samuel 1:3, **Shalom:** Our peace - Judges 6:24, **Elyon:** The Lord most high - Psalm 47:2, **Nissi:** Our banner - Exodus 17:15, **Ropheka**: our healer - Exodus 15:26, **Hoseenu**: our maker - Psalm 95:6, **Eloheeka**: Thy God - Exodus 20:7 **Mekaddisheem:** The Lord Our Sanctifier - Exodus 31:13, **Adonai:** our Sovereign - Genesis 15:2-8, **Rohi**: Our Shepherd, Psalm 23:1 **Jireh:** will provide Genesis 22:8-14, **Elohim**: our eternal creator Genesis 2:4-25.

You follow it with praises to Him for his benefits and promises provided in the New Covenant and what he has done for you.

Step Two: *Thy Kingdom come. Thy will be done on earth as it is in heaven.* Here Jesus taught us to establish and maintain priorities. What is the kingdom of God? The Kingdom of God is where God rules, governs and has divine standards full of grace (unmerited favour) that we have to follow. Romans 14:17 declares that, "the kingdom of God is not meat and drink, but righteousness, joy and peace in the Holy Ghost". Here you pray that God's rule, governance and presence which brings righteousness, joy and peace be established in the priorities that God has set over your life. Once your priorities are determined, you start praying about them, speaking eternal truths by the Holy Spirit on them. Things are moved when your tongue (your confession) agrees with your inner spirit, the course of life is set when it is in line with the word of God.

In 1 Corinthians 4:20, Paul states the Kingdom of God is manifest not in words but in power. This power also produces God's righteousness, joy and peace in our hearts, through the Holy Spirit (Romans 14.17). You pray that God's kingdom come and be established in the five major areas of life:

A. **Yourself**. Begin with yourself. Unless you are right before God, your prayers will not be effective. Prioritise to be in a right relationship with God by putting Him first, turning away from your sins and accepting His forgiveness and Lordship over your life. The Bible says "The effectual, fervent prayer of a righteous man avails much". (James 5:16). You confess your sin and pledge to the Lord, that you are not coming out of this time of prayer until God's Kingdom (His rule and purpose) comes in your life and His will be done in your life and to be set in your spirit.

You cannot properly administrate your home, business, resources and so forth, without God's help, divine wisdom and revelation. You should pray that God's Kingdom come in every area of your life. "His will be done as it is in heaven" Picture Jesus sitting on the throne of your spirit, soul and body. Set your mind in agreement with the will of God (the word) for your life; setting your affection on things above, not on earthly things; for you have died and your life is now hidden with Christ in God (Colossians 3:2-3).

B. Your Family. This is your second priority. If you are married pray for your spouse. Pray that righteousness, peace and joy will rule your spouse's life. Start making a declaration of faith that, the Lord's kingdom come and His Will be done over the life and needs of your spouse, until the Holy Spirit leads you to move on in prayer for your children.

Pray over the needs of your children if you have any. If they are married, pray for their children and the in-laws. If they are not married pray for their future partners. Commit their future into God's hand. Pray that the perfect will of God be done in their life. Pray for your children who are not Christians to come to the Lord to be saved.

C. Your Church. Pray for the pastor and the leaders of your church.   Pray for God to anoint them for the work of the ministry. Pray that God should speak and direct your pastor with regards to having a shepherd's heart. Pray that God would impart to him/her wisdom and strength to spend time in the word and in prayer through the help of the Holy Spirit.

Pray that God gives your pastor and his family, the strength to cope with church pressures and issues that arise. Pray that God would use them as a vessel to bless you spiritually and in the things of God. Pray for the leadership, the faithfulness of God's people, for fruitfulness and the harvest of souls, pray for the congregation also.

D. Your Work Place. Pray that God's will be done and established at your work place, His righteousness to be seen in the life of your organisation or establishment. Pray for the directors, managers and colleagues, as God uses you to be the salt of the earth and the light of the world (Matthew 5: 13-14) and also to act as a minister of reconciliation (I Corinthians 5:18) to others.

E. Your Nation. Pray for your national leaders, the President, the Prime Ministers, judges, Members of Parliament, the councilors, the law makers, for your cities and the towns that the kingdom of God comes and the will of God be established in their life, family, nation and in the land. Pray for God to give them wisdom and knowledge to lead their nations in the right way that pleases God, in order for us to live peaceful and quiet lives in all godliness and holiness. As the Bible says, the King's heart is in the hand of the Lord, like rivers of water, He directs it in whichever way He will and whenever He pleases. (Proverbs 21:1-3).

Step Three. *Give us this day our daily bread.* This precept gives us guidelines of how to pray and appropriate God's provisions. When praying for your needs, you must first of all be in the will of God. Secondly, you must believe that it is God's will to provide and prosper you. Thirdly, you must be specific in praying for what you need. And fourthly you must be tenacious in your prayers.

Being in the will of God implies (a) You must be in fellowship with Jesus through the reading and studying of the Word of God, obedient to his commands/words and to have a personal prayer life. (b) You must be in fellowship with God's church and His people. You must be diligent, with balanced work habits, and (d) you must be obedient in giving.

To put more emphasis on being in the will of God one has to be:

A. In the will of God, you must be in fellowship with Jesus through a consistent personal prayer life. Reading, meditating on and obeying the Word of God is very essential. Jesus warned His disciples, to watch and pray so as not fall into temptation. The spirit is willing but the flesh is weak (Matthew 26:41). James also said in James 1:25 "But whosoever look into the perfect law that gives freedom, and continues to do this, not forgetting what he has heard, but continues doing, he will be blessed in what he does". As we seek the Lord each day, the Holy Spirit empowers us with the ability, and might to do the will of God and to transform ourselves more and more into the image of God.

B. In fellowship with one another. We were commanded in Hebrews 10:25 not to give up meeting together, as some were in the habit of doing, but to encourage one another, all the more as we see the Day approaching. God is keen for us to be in fellowship with each other and other believers so as to build ourselves and others up because we are one body (1 Corinthians 12: 20, 21, 25, 26). We cannot say to another member of the body of Christ "I have no need of you".

This is also what the early Church did (Act 2:42), where the believers devoted themselves to the apostles' teaching and to fellowship with each other as well as to the breaking of bread and to prayer. Believers have to meet regularly to edify each other.

C. The third prerequisite for being in the will of God is to have diligent and balanced work habits (Genesis 2:15). When God created Man (Adam), He commissioned him to work. The Apostle Paul also instructs us in 1 Thessalonians 4:11,12, that we have to earn our living with our own hands in order to command the respect of the outside world, we are also to be self-supporting, and having need of nothing. He also commanded that "if anyone would not work neither should they eat." Therefore you should pray for the work you have been doing.

D. The last condition, to being in the will of God, is obedience in your giving to the Lord (Psalm 112:1, 2). Anyone who obeys the Lord is the one who can praise him. In verse 2, that person is blessed because he fears the Lord and he also finds delight in the Lord's command. Such people have faith, are obedient and they love the Lord.

You need a giving heart to remain in God's will. God commanded us to bring all our tithes into the storehouse that there may be food in His house. He will then open the window of heaven and pour out so much blessing that there will not be enough room for it (Malachi 3:10). We have to give to God's work on earth for His Kingdom on earth to expand and be fruitful (Luke 6:38). We were told by Jesus to give and it will be given to us, a good measure, pressed down, shaken together and running over will be poured to our lap, for with the same measure you use it will be measured to you. We must also seek the kingdom of God and His righteousness first, and all things shall be added unto us (Matthew 6:33). As God is our source, we cannot claim God's blessings if we violate this principle for prospering or blessing us.

We cannot have a poverty mentality and receive God's best if we waiver in faith. We have to believe that, it is God's will to prosper us, even as our soul enriches itself in him (3John 2). John affirmed and prayed that we have good health and all may go well with us, even as our soul prospers. Philippians 4:19 assures us our God will meet all our needs according to His glorious riches in Christ Jesus, if we are obedient to His will.

We must also be specific in our praying for God's provision when making our request "Give us this day our daily bread" (Matthew 6:4): Jesus wants us to pray daily over our specific needs. Paul also reminded us not to be anxious for anything but in everything by praying and supplication with thanksgiving we should let our request be made known to God (Philippians 4:6).

We must be very tenacious in praying for our needs, continuing to be persistent and full of faith, not doubting when requesting from God. We should not give up and be halfhearted (Luke 18:1). Jesus urges us to always pray and not to be fainthearted. Paul also encourages us to pray without ceasing in 1 Thessalonians 5:17.

We also have a brilliant promise in Hebrews 11:6 which states that without faith it is impossible to please God, for he that comes to God must believe that He is, and He is the rewarder of those who diligently seek Him.

Step Four: *Forgive us our debts, as we also have forgiven our debtors.* This step pinpoints and gives us the principles of God's standards and how to get along with everybody at all times. It is here that you bring your relationships and attitudes before the Lord in prayer.

- Ask God to forgive you. The word of God in 1 John 1:9 urges us to confess our sins to God, and He is faithful and just to cleanse us from all unrighteousness. God is ever ready to forgive us all our sins if we sincerely confess them to Him and turn back from them, because He has borne all our sins on the Cross (Isaiah 53:4-6).

- Forgive as often as you want to be forgiven. Jesus himself commanded us in Matthew 6:14, that we should forgive men when they sin against us and then our heavenly Father will also forgive us. If we do not forgive others who sin against us, our heavenly Father will not forgive our sins. Keeping unforgiveness, anger, bitterness, malice or hatred in our heart against others, obstructs us from approaching the presence of God and receiving His blessings.

These cords torment and rob you from your joy, peace and victory. Jesus warned in Matthew 5:23-24 that, when we are to offer our gifts at the altar and remember that we have something against a brother (verse 24), we should leave our gift in front of the altar, and go and be reconciled to our brother, before offering our gift (request, petition or offering) to God.

Peter asked Jesus (Matthew 18:21-22) "Lord, how many times shall I forgive my brother when he sins against me? Up to seven times?". Jesus answered "I tell you not seven times but seventy times seven". Jesus dismissed Peter's calculation. Our willingness to forgive should be limitless. We forgive because we have been forgiven by God and no offence against us can remotely compare with the incalculable amount of offences for which we have been forgiven.

Maintain a right attitude towards others. We have seen how important it is to have a forgiving attitude; but how can we have a right attitude towards everybody all the time, when people are hovering around us, waiting for us to fail or criticising us. In reality each of us have been sinned against, lied about, used, misused and abused in this life. The key to a right attitude is preparation. Do not wait until you are in the heat of emotional conflict to decide how you will react. You can be more gentle and loving. Be more concerned about the other person than yourself. The offender needs love and forgiveness and you need to forgive them. Do not allow your spirit to be robbed. Un-forgiveness breeds bitterness which takes root in your spirit. Ultimately it will steal your joy, peace, victory and eventually cause sickness or even death. Proverbs 4:23 warns us "Keep your heart with all diligence, for out of it flow the issues of life."

Step Five, *"And lead us not into temptation, but deliver us from evil,"* In this prayer topic Jesus teaches us how to protect ourselves and consistently defeat the Devil. It is vital for you to stand in the victory that Christ has won for you. Here, you build a hedge of protection around yourself, your loved ones and your possessions. We are also encouraged to put on the armor of light and defeat the Devil and his schemes.

A. Temptation: Our God cannot be tempted with evil, and He Himself tempts no man (James 1:13-14). Scripture also says that, everyone is tempted, when he is drawn away of his own lust, and enticed. However, Jesus teaches us to pray, "Lead us not into temptation" (Matthew 6:13). Who is the tempter that Jesus is referring to?

The Devil is the tempter (Matthew 4:3 and 1 Thessalonians 3:5). The scriptures warn us of temptations which come from the Devil (Matthew 4:1; 1 Corinthians 5:5). Paul reveals that even strong Christians are vulnerable to temptation (Galatians 6:1). The origin for temptation may vary. Some temptations or trials arise from within, from uncontrolled appetites, evil passions or our own lust (Mark 7:20-22; James 1:13-14). Temptations from within or from Satan does not proceed from God, He does observe His people while they endure it, and through the temptation He makes a way out for them and affirms them. We have to pray that the Holy Spirit will help, guide and strengthen us so we do not fall into temptation. Nevertheless, scriptures reveal in 1 Corinthians 10:13 that "No temptation has seized us except what is common to man, and since God is faithful, he will not let you be tempted beyond what you can bear, however when you are tempted, He will make a way out so that you can stand up to it". 2 Peter 2:9 also assures us that The Lord knows how to rescue godly men from trials and to hold the unrighteous for the day of judgement, when they will face their punishment. Temptations and trials teach us spiritual warfare.

B. Deliver us from the evil one. We need the help of the Holy Spirit's power to deliver us from the evil one. The apostle Paul urges us, in Ephesians chapter 6:10-17, of how to apply the whole armour of God.

What the armour is: It is the character and attributes of God himself. Putting on the whole armour of God as mentioned in Ephesians 6:10-17 is the application and manifestation of Jesus Christ in our daily life.

We have to put on the full armour of God every day. Jesus is the whole armour of God. **Let's discover Jesus briefly in the armour listed in Ephesians 6: 14-17. First,** verse 14. "We have to have our waist guarded with the truth". Who is your truth? It is Jesus Christ. He said "I am the way, the truth and the life (John 14:6). **Secondly,** "having put on the breastplate of righteousness", who is your righteousness? It is Jesus. You have no righteousness of your own. Only by the blood of Jesus are you covered with the free gift of righteousness. Jesus Christ himself. **Thirdly,** Verse 15 "With your feet shod with the preparation of the gospel of peace". What is the preparation of the gospel of peace? The gospel is that Jesus Christ died for our sins, according to the scriptures, was buried and rose again on the third day to forgive, save us and give us eternal life. The word preparation means readiness to walk in the gospel of peace and also the ability to walk in the Spirit of God, just as Jesus did (1 Peter 3:15). We have to set apart the Lord in our heart and be ready to give answer to everyone who asks us a reason for our hope that is in Jesus Christ, with meekness and fear. The good news of Jesus Christ brings peace (Romans 5:1). Being justified by faith, we have peace with God through Jesus Christ. God gives us a peace which goes beyond our understanding (Philippians 4:7). **Fourthly,** Verse 16 "In addition take up the shield of faith". Who is your faith? Nobody but Jesus! Who else produces faith in your life? As you take in and hear the word of God, the Spirit of God comes into your heart to produce the faith needed to believe for the things of God. He is the author and finisher of our faith (Hebrew 12:2). **Fifthly,** "Take the helmet of salvation" who is your salvation today? It is Jesus Christ, and in the same verse, it says "and the sword of the Spirit", which is the word of God. Who is the word of God? It is Jesus Christ (John 1:1-2) "In the beginning was the Word, and the Word was with God, and the Word was God. He was in the beginning with God". Paul encouraged us to be strong in the Lord and in His mighty power.

To be strong in the Lord means to be praying fervently with the help of the Holy Spirit and, to be alert and watchful. We need to rely on God's power, strength and on His Spirit, not our own strength. Paul goes on to say that in order to do that, we should put on the full armour of God so that we can stand against the Devil's schemes. Putting on the full armour of God every day, is when we are able to stand firm against any tricks or cunning of the devil. The reverse of that is, if you do not put on the whole armour of God, you will not be able to stand against tricks, craftiness and slyness of the Devil. Paul instructs us in (Romans 13:12,14) to put aside the deeds of darkness and to put on the armour of light and also to clothe ourselves with the Lord Jesus Christ, by obeying, adhering to and using the Word of God daily in our life.

The armour Paul is talking about here is, in reality the Lord Jesus Christ. Jesus is our defender (1 John 2:1). He wants to be our defence and to clothe ourselves with himself. The armour was compared with the armour of a Roman soldier.

Paul instructed us in Ephesians 6:13 "wherefore by putting on the whole armour of God we are able to stand our ground when the day of evil comes". After you have done everything with regards to putting on the armour (God's armour) you continue to stand. Later on, Paul went on to define that armour in detail.

1. Stand, therefore, with the belt of truth buckled around the waist.

The waist, or loins are that part of the body between the ribs and the hipbones. This part signifies the seat of physical strength and generative power. The digestive system, reproductive organs and the bowel (which eliminate waste) are contained here. We are to desire the truth of God's Word in our inward and hidden parts of our being. The Psalmist said in Psalm 51:6, "Surely you desire truth in the inner part and teach me wisdom in the inmost place". In God's covenant He made with the people of Israel, God declared in Jeremiah 31:33 "I will put my law in their inward parts and write it in their hearts, I will be their God and they will be my people". Jesus is the way, the truth and the life (John 14:6). He has to be our truth in and around our loins. We need to have an inner conviction and stand on the side of truth. The objective truth of God's Word keeps the believer strong and victorious, in spiritual conflict and warfare.

2. With the breastplate of righteousness in place.

The breastplate is a piece of armour worn over the chest. It protects the vital organs of life with in us, the heart, oesophagus and lungs. In spiritual terms, these would represent the important parts of the human soul like the heart, will, emotions. Paul reminds us in 1 Thessalonians 5:8 "to be self-controlled, putting on faith and love as a breastplate and hope of salvation as a helmet". I Corinthians 1:30 assures us that we have been made the righteousness of God in Jesus Christ. Believers must make every effort to be obedient to God, to put their trust in Jesus and to walk in righteousness with Him by faith. In prayer remind yourself of your righteousness by God through faith (1Corinthians 1:30). In Proverbs 4:23, we are urged to guard our hearts with all diligence, for out of it flow the issues of life.

3. And your feet shod with the preparation of the gospel of peace.

Our feet have the ability to stand, walk and run etc.; they are very vital. Our feet need to be firmly stabilised with the gospel, in order for us to stand and deal victoriously with the enemy's device and tactics in spiritual conflict. Paul instructs us to prepare our feet with the readiness that comes from the gospel of peace, in order for our words and actions to be firm and steadfast, not distracted, always abounding in the work of the Lord and ready for spiritual warfare. The scriptures tell us in Psalm 18:33 "He makes our feet like the feet of a deer and enables us to stand on the heights". The Lord enables us by the help of the Holy Spirit, to stand firm and to make progress on the dangerous heights of testing and trouble, in order to bring the gospel of peace everywhere that our feet tread. Also be ready to share the gospel of peace with others. Scripture assures us to make peace with God and with everyone (Romans 5:1) and (Romans 12:18).

4. Take up the shield of faith

In addition to all this, take up the shield of faith, with which you can extinguish all the flaming arrows of the evil one. The shield was a piece of the armour carried on the arm or in the hand to protect the entire body in battle. It is used in every direction that the enemy throws arrows or darts. Proverbs 30:5 states "Every word of God is flawless, He is a shield to those who take refuge in Him". We need to positively and faithfully hold on to God's promises revealed in the gospel by faith and also be able to use it appropriately when the enemy throws vain imagination, evil desires and temptation against us. Furthermore we are to use the word of God in faith to deter every terror by night and the arrow that flies by day (Psalm 91:5)., (Using the word of God by faith as Jesus did in these verses (Matthews 4:4-10), defeats every dart and arrow the devil throws at us, whether it is doubt, vain imagination, unbelief or lust. The word of God is quick and powerful and sharper than any two-edged sword. The word revealed to us becomes a weapon in our mouth if we declare it by faith.

5. Take the helmet of Salvation...

The helmet was worn to protect the head. One vital organ in our head is the brain. The brain controls the whole body, and is that part which we use to operate the mind.

The Psalmist also said in Psalm 140:7 "O God my Lord, the strength of my salvation, you have covered my head in the day of battle". We need to be transformed by the renewing of our mind by the word of God (Romans 12:2) and (Ephesians 4:23). In order for us to have full assurance of salvation and not to be deceived when the enemy comes against us with doubt, unbelief, fear, vain imaginations, discouragement and negative thoughts in our mind, we need to be able to stand and act on the assurance of the word of God. We need to protect our minds in order for Satan not to contaminate our soul and spirit (1 Corinthians 7:1), and for us to have full assurance of our salvation based on the conviction of the Holy Spirit and the word of God, in order for us not to lose heart and lose our faith.

All the pieces of the entire armour have been designed for defence and protection. However the sword of the Spirit which is the word of God, is the only piece of armour, designed to be both a defensive and an offensive weapon.

6. And the sword of the Spirit, which is the word of God.

The sword is a weapon with a sharp blade on one or both sides, fixed in a handle or hilt. Used to kill or wound, it is usually wielded with the right arm. The sword is a symbol of power and authority.

Our sword which symbolises power and authority is **the word of God**. Psalm 149:6 states "Let the high praises of our God be in their mouth and a two-edged sword in their hand". We also read in Hebrews 4:12 that "For the word of God is living, quick, powerful and sharper than any two - edged sword, piercing and dividing the soul and spirit, and of the joints and marrow. It is a discerner of the thoughts and intents of the heart". To use the word of God in prayer is **key**. God wants us to use the word of God to defeat and resist every wile of the enemy, after we have submitted ourselves to Him (James 4:7). The devil throws doubt at God's word, at his promises and commandments in our mind and heart in order to sidetrack us from doing the will of God, and we need the power of God's word to counteract the enemy. Like Jesus's example in Matthew 4:4-10 when tempted by Satan, Jesus answered and referred to the pure and flawless word of God (it is written he quoted the word of God) against Satan's temptations. Jesus knew that the living word of God is the most powerful weapon against the temptation of the devil. If Jesus himself uses the word of God to counter the devil, do we dare to use anything less?

Truth, righteousness, helmet of salvation, readiness of the gospel of peace, shield of faith and **the word of God** must be empowered by prayer and supplication in the spirit for maximum effectiveness. We must keep alert and be persistent as we pray for our brothers, sisters in Christ and the church. After Apostle Paul has described all the armour, he added the last piece of armour "Praying always with all prayer and supplication in the Spirit and watching with all perseverance and supplication for all the saints (Ephesians 6:18). Being alert and always watching and praying in any other language and the language of the Spirit. Moreover, Jude 20 encourages us to build ourselves in our most holy faith by praying in the Holy Spirit. In 1 Corinthians 14:2 Paul urges us that for anyone who speaks in a tongue, does not speak to men but to God. Indeed, no one understands him, but he utters mysteries in the Spirit. Verse 14 reads, if we pray in a tongue, our spirit prays, but our understanding is unfruitful. We have to pray in the spirit often and more to go deeper in the things of God (Spiritual realm).

Having put on all the armour, we have to stand. If we do not put on the whole armour of God, we cannot stand against the wiles of the devil and we will not be able to withstand in the day of evil. The day of evil is any day that the enemy comes in like a flood.

Every Christian should be involved in spiritual warfare. This shall not be an option, but a requirement for all Christians because we are constantly engaged in the spiritual battle with the devil. God is seeking an army of intercessors who will stand and raise their hands in prayer and praise, to poke holes in the kingdom of darkness.

Jesus is found in the believer- in you and in me.

Build a hedge of protection: We always have to declare a hedge of protection around ourselves, our family, our church, work, business and possessions. God has put a hedge of protection on his righteous ones, their household and their possessions (Job 1: 10). The Psalmist reminds us in Psalm 91:1-2 that "He who dwells in the shelter of the Most High will rest in the shadow of the Almighty. I will say of the Lord He is my refuge and my fortress, in Whom I trust".

God already protects us if we abide in Him. There are 3 reasons why we have to declare a hedge of protection, which can be seen in Psalm 91:9-14. Because a) You have made the Most High your dwelling b) He loves you c) You acknowledge His name.

Step Six: *"For thine is the Kingdom and the power and the glory forever"* In this precept Jesus pinpoints on how to obey the word's most dynamic commandment. The Lord's Prayer starts and ends with praise. We have brought our petitions to the throne of grace. We need to give him thanks for his blessings and now we return to praise in this last prayer mark.

WHEN WE ARE TO PRAISE:

The Psalmist David knew the importance of praising the Lord when He had granted David's victory and the battle was over.

We must not forget to praise the Lord for His deliverance, victory and faithfulness to us.

We are to praise God continually and in all things; in times of rest and peace, when souls are won, in the midst of trials and even when the trial is on and over. In fact some battles are won through praise (2 Chronicles 20: 1-30). Jehoshaphat's victory over his enemies. The wall of Jericho fell down through the power of praise (Joshua Chapter 6:12-20).

A. Praise continually:

We are encouraged in the book of Hebrews 13:15; "Through Jesus, therefore, let us continually offer to God a sacrifice of praise, the fruit of our lips that confess His name" We are to praise God continually and in all things. To praise God for what he has done, what He is doing and what He will do. The writer also stated in Hebrews 13.8 that "He is the same yesterday, today and forever."

B. Praise when our souls are at rest:

We need to praise God when there are no storms, when there is a storm, going through the storms, and after the storm, and when our souls are at rest. The Psalmist David knew this secret, he said in Psalm 32:7 that "You are my hiding place. You will protect me from trouble, and surround me with songs of deliverance".

C. Praise in the midst of trials and trouble:

In everything give thanks, for this is the will of God in Christ Jesus concerning you (1 Thessalonians 5:18). As a child of God, you have to praise God in every situation for this is the will of God concerning you. It might be that God is testing your faith, He wants you to go through a learning process, He wants to change you for the better, or it might be that He wants to bless you and your blessing is near.

Paul and Silas were thrown in prison, and at midnight they sang praises to God. Their chains were then loosed when a violent earthquake shook the foundation. Through this event a jailer was saved and then they were set free by the local magistrate the next morning (Acts 16:25-26).

In the midst of trial, Jonah repented and praised the Lord for his deliverance (Jonah 2:7-10).

King Jehoshaphat and the people of Judah sang praises to God at the time of battle against Ammon and Moab and the Lord delivered them (2 Chronicles 20:1-30).

D. Praise when trials are over:

The words of the Psalmist David again encourage us in Psalm 40:2, to praise God when we are out of trouble and when our trials are over. David said "He brought me up out of a horrible pit and the miry clay and set my feet upon a rock and established my going."

RETURN TO PRAISE:

Jesus's model of prayer points us towards His Kingdom, His Power and His Glory forever. In scripture we learn that God has faithfully and lovingly invited us to be participants in His Kingdom, His Power and His glory(2 Peter 1:3-4). So Jesus instructs us to return to Praise.

Thine is the Kingdom. In Psalm 22:28 we are assured of this by declaring that "For the kingdom is the Lord's". The Lord also promises us in Luke 12:32 that "We should not be afraid, little flock, because it is the Father's pleasure to give us the kingdom". The Kingdom of God belongs to the Lord and us. We need also to give thanks and praise to the Father who has qualified us to share in the inheritance of the saints in the Kingdom of Light (1Peter 1:3-4); "For the Lord has rescued us from the dominion of darkness and brought us into the kingdom of his son whom he loves" (Colossians 1:12-13). The Lord will always rescue us from every evil attack and bring us safely to his heavenly Kingdom (2 Timothy 4:18).

Thine is the Power. God upholds power in His mighty strength and He needs to be exalted for that. Psalm 21:13 encourages us to exalt the Lord in His strength, to sing to him and to praise His might. He rules forever by His power (Psalm 66:7). God sustains His kingdom by His power. Without His power nothing can be sustained or can remain on the earth. Scriptures made us know in Jeremiah 10:12 that God made the earth by his power He founded the world by his wisdom and stretched out the heavens by his understanding. God desires praise from his people for what he has done and what he can do and as well as for his power, wisdom and understanding.

Thine is the glory. All divine attributes belong to God. He declares in scripture, through the Prophet Isaiah in Isaiah 42:8, that - I am the Lord that is my name. I will not share my glory with another or share my praise to an idol. We can take nothing from God's glory, but He has invited us to be participants of his glory, even though all men have fallen short of the glory of God (Romans 3:23). God manifested perfection in his character. David, in the book of Psalms 24:8 asks us "Who is this King of Glory? The Lord, strong and mighty, the Lord, mighty in battle."

Know this truth - God's Kingdom, His power and His glory is forever!

The book of Revelation tells us who all this kingdom, power and glory belongs to, because Revelation 5:13 reads "praise and honour, glory and power, be unto Him (God) who sits upon the throne, and unto the lamb forever and ever".

Thine is the Kingdom: thine is the power: thine is the glory: May we never enter or leave His presence without humbling ourselves before Him and offering a sacrifice of praise.

CHAPTER 9

PRAYERS IN THE NEW TESTAMENT

Throughout the gospels, Jesus taught his disciples how to pray (Matthew 6:5-14), and he gave them parables with regard to prayers (Luke 11:1-13), (Luke 18: 1-8). His disciples witnessed him pray and do miracles, healing the sick (Mark 7:31-35), (8:22-26), casting out demons, (Matthew 8:28-34) (Matthew 9:27-29), raising the dead (John 11:33-44), (Luke 8:49-56). To name a few, all of these were done through different kinds of prayers offered up by Jesus. Some of his prayers were witnessed by the disciples.

During the early years of the Christian Church, the whole subject of prayer was central. Amid sporadic and at times intense persecution, the purpose of prayer was explored and a journey began to emerge from the writings of the early disciples.

After the risen and resurrected Lord had given the disciples **(you are a disciple of Jesus if you believe in him and have confessed him as your Lord and personal saviour)** instruction and promise and after having impacted them by his power and teachings, their faith and expectation increased (Act1:1-11).

Acts 1:14. The disciples continued with one accord, constantly in **prayer** and supplication.

Acts 2:1-4, 14-41. They were still in the **prayer meeting** when the Holy Spirit fell on them. The disciples continued to pray, which resulted in the place being shaken up, and they all spoke with other tongues as the Spirit enabled them. You would notice that on the day of Pentecost, the disciples were in one accord, in one Spirit, and of one attitude in prayer. They were not studying, not having church meeting, leaders or board meeting, they were not sermonising, they were not memorising bible verses and slogans, **they were praying!** When the power and glory of God broke through, signs, wonders and salvation followed, after Peter had preached the word of God, this resulted in 3,000 souls who believed, were baptised and were then subsequently added to the church (verse 41).

Acts 3:1-11, Peter and John were going up to the temple at the **time of prayer,** at three in the afternoon, when they healed the lame man at the gate called Beautiful. After a **time of prayer, Acts** 3:1, Peter boldly preached his second sermon and many of them who heard the word of God believed; and the number of men were about 5,000 although the women and children were not counted. The prayer Peter and John prayed resulted in healing and the power of God on them to win souls to the kingdom. (Act: 4:1-22)

Acts 4: 23-31, After the apostles/disciples were arrested and threatened by the Jewish authorities, Peter and John went back and raised their voices **together in prayer** to God (prayer meeting). This was not a board meeting or a Council of Deacons but a **prayer meeting**. The result: after prayers, the place where they were assembled together, shook and they were all filled with the Holy Spirit and they spoke the word of God with boldness.

Acts 5:12-15 all the believers used to meet together in Solomon's colonnade. On this occasion they met together in one accord in Solomon's colonnade (I believe they must have been praying and worshipping before this as it produced results) the apostles performed many signs and wonders among the people and many more believed. Men and women were added to the Church and many were also healed.

Acts 6:4-7 the disciples gave themselves totally to the **ministry of prayer** and the word of God. As a direct result, the word of God grew and the number of disciples in Jerusalem also grew rapidly and multiplied. Even a large number of religious Priests became obedient to the faith and were converted.

Acts 7: 59-60 in this instance, Stephen, the first Christian martyr, **prayed that** God would forgive his executors as he died. I am convinced that the prayers of this Spirit- filled, dying saint, full of God's grace and power, produced the greatest apostle. For example Paul, who was holding the clothes of the mob that stoned Stephen, was converted in Acts chapter 9.

Acts 8:14-17 the disciples sent Peter and James to Samaria to **pray** for the Saints to receive the Holy Spirit.

Acts 9 In an answer to Stephen's prayer, Saul, who was one of his executors, was apprehended by God on his way to Damascus. He received his mandate from God and stayed without food and water for three days as he desperately sought the face of God in **prayer**. Ananias also laid his hands on Saul, prayed for him to receive his sight, to be filled with the Holy Spirit and Saul was baptized. However, prior to Saul's conversion in chapter 9, chapter 8 tells us that as a result of what had happened whereby Saul had persecuted the Church, this had resulted in an increase of believers and a subsequent expansion of the Church through the intense prayers offered by the believers to God.

Acts 9:40-42 Peter **prayed** for Tabitha and she was raised from the dead. As a result of this miracle, many people believed in the Lord.

Acts10:9, Peter goes to the rooftop of the house to **pray** about the sixth hour. The outcome was that Peter fell into a trance and received a vision from the Lord. He preached the word of God to Cornelius which led to the conversion of Cornelius and his family. Many other gentiles, also received the gift of the Holy Spirit, and were baptized as well as the believers.

Acts 12:5, 12, Peter the leader of the apostolic band, was arrested. God intervened and Peter was freed as a result of the church praying earnestly to God for Peter. Miracles happened because, despite the persecution, the church experienced the atmosphere of the power of God through prayer and continued to grow.

Acts 13: 1-3, while the leaders of the church at Antioch were waiting on God in **worship, prayer and fasting,** the Holy Spirit instructed them to separate Saul and Barnabas for the ministry to which He had called them to bring light to the Gentiles. This was their missionary call to the ministry.

Acts 14:21-23 After the gospel had been preached to a large number of disciples in Lystra, Paul and Barnabas strengthened and encouraged the disciples to remain true to the faith. These two apostles (Paul and Barnabas) then appointed elders in each church, and with **prayer and fasting,** committed them to the Lord.

Acts 16:13-34 The first convert in Europe, Lydia was converted by the Holy Spirit, through Paul, in a **prayer meeting and an open gospel outreach**. Also from verse 16, Paul and Silas were on their way to a **prayer meeting** when they drove out a spirit of divination from a slave girl. This resulted in Paul and Silas being stripped, beaten and put in prison. Despite this, verse 25 states that at midnight they **prayed** and sang praises to the Lord. Even the other prisoners heard them and suddenly, there was a violent earthquake. The foundation of the prison shook, their chains became loosed, and the prison door opened. After witnessing this miracle and the power of God, the jailer and his household received Christ as their Saviour and Lord and they were baptized. There is often a greater intervention of God when He responds to the effectual fervent prayers of His people.

The message is clear. The early church had multiplication of growth and breakthrough because they had grasped the importance of prayer, the miracles they were witnessing, the healings and conversion of souls because they had given prayer a priority. **That is the key**. Prayer should be a priority before the day starts, during the day, at the end of the day and for it to be a way of life.

CHAPTER 10

PRAYERFUL MEN IN CHURCH HISTORY

God throughout history has worked through men and women of prayer!

Let us see some of the Fathers of faith throughout Church History who accomplished great work for God by the power of prayer.

George Muller, man of faith and prayer (1801-1900)

George Muller originated from Germany but resided in England. He turned his life to Christ at a small prayer meeting with hymns. It was a real turning point for George. He felt the call of God upon his life after a cloud of pure joy experience bubbling within him. He no longer desired to have a comfortable parish home, but he wanted to do mission work and with his decision, he immediately received the peace of God that passes all understanding.

George changed the way Church charges rent for pews to listen to the gospel praying and trusting God.

George prayed intensive prayers to God for the need of providing bibles to local day schools and adult schools for his homeland and abroad.

George Muller's walk with God was that he believed God would answer his prayers and God did answer George.

Once, Muller prayed successfully for a fog to disappear during a ship trip. He also prayed that there should be an ample supply of provisions to his orphanage that he built at a time of financial difficulty and God answered his prayers.

John Knox (1514-1572) was a great Scottish reformer. A Minister and a theologian, John was a leader in the country's reformation. He was the founder of the Presbyterian Church of Scotland. He learnt the lent of God breakthrough and he was effective in prayer. John Knox had a passion for renewal in Scotland and he formed the Presbyterian Church where he built prayerful men in his ministry, training up leaders who were fruitful in ministry. All through this, he was consistent in prayers both inprivate and public.

This is how to facilitate God breakthrough in situations.

John Knox once prayed Lord. "Give me Scotland or I will die" Frankly, he got Scotland and way beyond as more souls were added to God's kingdom through his prayers and ministry. Praise God.

Robert Bruce: (1554 - 1631)

Robert Bruce was a Minister of the gospel in Scotland. A lot of people flocked to hear his sermons. His preaching was very powerful for several reasons: In his reverence for God as he always gave priority to God the Saviour, in his preaching. Robert viewed himself as nothing more, yet nothing less than an ambassador of Jesus Christ. He was also sincere. His aim was to be always faithful to his Divine Master's words and to profit the soul of his hearers. Robert's method of preparation also helped him to access the power of the Holy Spirit so that he could preach powerful messages to his hearer for edification. He devoted himself to diligent study and earnest prayers.

Coupled with a deep study of Holy Scripture was Bruce's earnest prayer for the presence of God in his preaching. Jesus Christ must be present by His Spirit, in the hearts of the hearers. The hearers must enjoy the presence of Jesus Christ by His Spirit.

John Wesley and Charles Wesley:

John Wesley was born at Bridport, Dorset, the son of the Rev. Batholomew and Ann Colley. He was educated at Dorchester Grammar School and was a student of New Inn Hall. John Wesley was matriculated on 23rd April 1651 and graduated B.A. on 23rd January 1655. He was an English Cleric, Theologian, and an Evangelist. He lived and pursued a devout Christian life.

Wesley argued for the notion of Christian perfection and against Calvinism and in particular against its doctrine of predestination. He also pursued a rapidly methodical and abstemious life, studied the scriptures and performed his religious duties diligently, depriving himself so that he would have alms to give. He began to seek after Holiness of heart and consistent prayer life.

Charles Wesley was the junior brother of John Wesley who took on the study group in John's absence. Both men pursued a devoted Christian life and studied scriptures. Charles Wesley formed a small group purposefully to study the Holy Scriptures. They committed themselves daily from six (6) until nine (9) for prayers, Psalms and reading of the Greek New Testament. They prayed every waking hour for several minutes and each day for a special virtue. They fasted Wednesdays and Fridays until 3'oclock, visited prisoners in jail, and relieved jailed debtors.

Through the regular prayers of these two brothers with rigorous fasting, the Methodist Church which they formed was influenced, expanded by Wesley's deep faith and Spirituality rooted in Pietism.

Charles G. Finney (1792-1875)

Charles Finney is often called The American Revivalist. Finney led over a hundred thousand persons to Christ as a result of his labour. Charles Finney was an intense man who brought revival to churches in many communities of the northwest of

America. He promoted and taught about conversion, baptism of the Holy Spirit, promoting revival through the role of prayer, restitution, working with people of all class. He did not write his sermons on time but would study and pray over the topic and deliver the sermon powerfully to bring salvation, deliverance and healing to his audience. This Godly gifting with effective powerful prayers helped Charles Finney to cause revival in America Church History.

THE POWER OF PRAYER

The church was born in a **prayer meeting** (Acts 2).

When the people of God pray, the atmosphere is **shaken** (Acts 4:31 Acts 16:26).

Unceasing prayer will set the captives **free** (Acts 12).

Father, we need more of this today.

We have seen that, in the book of Acts, the disciples were prayerful throughout the early church, including the Apostle Paul. Paul who wrote most of the New Testament, had established and was also the overseer and apostle of most of the early churches. He was very prayerful. Paul prayed always for the churches: for the Ephesian church (Ephesians I: 16-19) for the Philippian church (Philippians 1:4-5) for the Colossian church (Colossians 1:3-4) as well as for the Thessalonian church (I Thessalonians 1:2-3) & (2 Thessalonians 1:3). Apostle Paul urges us in 1 Thessalonians 5:17 to pray without ceasing. He would not have told us this, if he was not a prayerful person.

Will you take up the challenge? Is God calling you? If you do, you will see the move of God in your life, your family life, your work, your church and in your nation because prayer changes things. Let me tell you there is no higher calling. When you pray, you have reached the throne. Others may not see you because you will be out of sight beyond the second view, but your life will count for God for time and eternity.

Father, pour on us your Spirit of grace and supplication.

CHAPTER 11

PRINCIPLES OF EFFECTIVE PRAYER

In James 5:16-18, we are encouraged as to how and when our prayers could be effective and produce results. In the preceding verses, verse 13 of James 5 asks if any of you is in trouble. We should pray. Is anyone happy? Let him sing songs of praise. Is anyone sick? He should call the elders of the church to pray over him and anoint him with oil in the name of the Lord and the prayer offered in faith will make the sick person well. The Lord will raise him up. If he has sinned, he will be forgiven. "Therefore confess your sins to each other and pray for each other, so that you may be healed".

In verse 16, it also says, the effectual fervent prayer of a righteous man is **powerful and effective**. In verse 17 it shows that Elijah was a man just like us. He prayed earnestly that it did not rain on the land for three and half years, again he prayed, and the heavens gave rain, and the earth produced its crops. This is exactly what we want our prayers to be like, especially in a time of crisis. When we meet God's requirement, we can be confident that He will not only hear our concerns but will act on them in accordance with His will and purposes.

To meet God's requirement we must be fervent, prayerful, as well as living and walking righteously.

1. Fervent prayer. Fervent prayer should be motivated by a deeply burdened heart. Fervent prayers are filled with passion and a strong sense of personal helplessness, but are trusting and depending on God's mighty ability. You also have to have a narrow focus on some specific difficulty, about which you care deeply. Scripture calls this type of prayer 'labouring earnestly'! An example is Epaphras in Colossians 4:12 who prays earnestly for the Colossian church to come to maturity and completeness in the will of God,

2. Righteousness: When we place our trust in the Lord, we become rightly related to God as His children. At that moment we are permanently sealed with the Holy Spirit and declared righteous forever because of our position in Jesus Christ (1 Corinthians 1:30). However, we have to live and walk right with God (Philippians 3:9). While salvation is by faith rather than deeds (Ephesians 2:8-9), genuine faith will result in an obedient lifestyle and good works (James 2:26). If we willingly and knowingly engage in sin, then we are not living righteously and our prayers will not be effective.

When the Lord hears an impassioned prayer, He knows who is

praying. If it is a righteous person whose life reflects God's ways, the Bible promises that the Holy Spirit will begin His divine work.

God responds with great power to the prayers of even one righteous person. That person could be you.

For our prayers also to be effective, we must **confess our sins** to God and to one another in particular, when we want to be healed. This has already been stated previously, in (James 5:16 -18).

We must also be **specific** in our prayer needs to God and not keep on babbling like the pagans as Jesus told us in Matthews 6:7.

We should pray with a sense of **need**, because we need God. We need God's Help.

We have to be **tenacious** in our prayers by keeping a firm hold of the promises of God and by being persistent in what we are praying about (Luke 11: 5-13 & Luke 18:1-8).

We must let our prayers be **intensive**. We must show eagerness, great warmth and depth in what we are praying about. An example would be Jesus praying in the Garden of Gethsemane (Luke 22:41-44), the disciples during the day of Pentecost (Acts 2:2), when Peter, John and a believer prayed in Acts 4:24-31, when the church was praying for Peter after his arrest (Acts 12:5).

There is a mighty difference between saying prayers and praying. Quotes John G. Lake.

Lastly, for your prayers to be effective you have to **pray in faith** (Mark 11:22-24) and (Hebrews 1:6).

Our problem is not that God is saying a loving no to many of our requests, it is that our prayers too often lack the depth that heaven requires. They seems to come from the head, not the heart. Instead of being propelled from our Spirit towards God with earnestness and faith that can not be denied.

They often wobble from uncertain lips and fall helpless to the father.

THE PERSONAL PRAYER LIFE

The development of an effective and consistent prayer life is not easy. Laziness, lack of discipline, distraction and demonic interference all play their part in seeking to undermine our most noble attempts. However a prayer life with a real power and significance is not beyond the reach of any Christian. We need desire and discipline, which then leads to delight.

CHAPTER 12

WHAT HINDERS OUR PRAYERS

Communion with God is the highest activity of which people are capable. The bible's doctrine of prayer however, emphasises God's character and the necessity of being in the right covenant relationship with Him (John 4:24). God does not therefore automatically "hear" every prayer. Some prayers are ineffective and useless. Isaiah 1:15 states that "When you spread out your hands in prayer, I will hide my face from you; even if you offer many prayers, I will not listen because your hands are full of blood". In Job 27:8-9; 35:13, Isaiah 59:2, Micah 3:4 and Luke 18:10-14 we see the type of prayers that achieve little or nothing. How solemn this truth is.

Consider the following obstacles when our prayers achieve little or nothing.

1. Sin & un-confessed sin: Sin is a violation of what God's glory demands (Romans 8:7). The most common definition of sin in the Old Testament is missing the mark or deviating from the goal or God's standard. The general New testament term is missing the target or deviating from the road as in John 8:46. One reason why we do not get our prayers answered by God is explained by what David the Psalmist said in Psalm 66:18 that "if I cherished sin in my heart, The Lord would not have listened". Sin is like leprosy or cancer. It spreads through your whole spirit, soul and body. Isaiah 59:1-2 emphasises that "the arm of the Lord is not too short to save us nor his ear too dull to hear, but your iniquities have separated you from your God." This signals that our lawlessness, or wickedness, stands between God and us. Our Holy God hates sin. He turns his face from sin and therefore will not hear our prayers except when we sincerely and remorsefully repent and confess our sin to God.

2. Any unforgiving in our heart. The second factor that hinders our prayers is not forgiving others in our heart. In Matthew 6:12-15 Jesus speaks about forgiveness and teaches his disciples about prayer. If you forgive men when they sin against you, then your heavenly father will also forgive you, however, if you do not forgive men their sins, your Father in heaven will not forgive your sins. That means not forgiving others in our hearts is of great concern to God, and before coming to Him, He wants us to get rid of it.

Not forgiving others in your heart blocks God's blessings towards you and hinders His response to your prayers. Jesus reminds us, (Matthew 5:23-24) that if we are offering our gift at the altar and we remember that our brother has done something against us, (verse 24) then we should leave our gift in front of the altar, go and resolve the conflict and be reconciled to our brother and then we can come and offer our gift. Mark 11:25 also commands us that "when you stand praying, if you hold anything against anyone, forgive him, so that your Father in heaven may forgive you your sins."

Holding un-forgiveness breeds bitterness, anger, sickness to our soul and, sometimes eventually death. We have to purify our hearts by releasing any un-forgiveness in our heart, against anyone who may have sinned against us or those we have sinned against. Let forgiveness reign in our hearts and let us make a conscious effort to forgive others, not retaining any malice or hate in our hearts before offering our prayers, gifts and sacrifices to God.

3. The third hindrance to prayer is **disobedience to God:** if we disobey God's Word, His direction, rebuke and discipline, this hinders our prayer since we are not in His will. Repent! Proverbs 1:23-26 states that "if you had responded to my rebuke, the Lord God would pour out his heart and thoughts to you". Verse 24 of Proverbs 1 says because you have rejected the Lord God when he called, He will laugh and mock at your disaster and calamity. When we disobey God's commandment and His word, He turns His face from us. We need to obey God absolutely in His word. There needs to be a repentance and rededication of your will to be restored to God again in fellowship (1John 1:9).

4. The fourth hindrance to prayer is **not abiding in Jesus and**

his word. Jesus made a profound statement in John 15:7 "that if you abide in me and my words abide in you, you shall ask what you will and it shall be done unto you. You need a relationship

with the Lord and to abide in His word. Being in His word, believing and acting on His word in your heart, then whatever you ask will be done for you, as you have a consistent relationship with him. Praying and abiding in the word of God will facilitate answers to prayer. If you do not abide in Jesus and his word, your prayer will be hindered and not be as effective.

5. Unbelief is the fifth hindrance to our prayers being answered. The Bible tells us in Hebrews 11:6 that without faith it is impossible to please God, he that comes to God must believe that He exists and that He is the rewarder of those who diligently seek him. Unbelief does not allow you to experience the blessing God has for you, but by believing and having faith in Him, He opens up his word by the Holy Spirit for His light to shine in your heart so that you hold on to the Covenant promises in His written word. We are urged, in Mark 11:22-25 to "Have faith in God". In this discourse, Jesus tells us, "I tell you the truth, if anyone says to the mountain be removed and cast into the sea, and does not doubt in his heart but believes that what he says will happen, it will be done for him. Therefore I tell you, whatever you ask for in prayer, believe that you have received it, and it will be yours" The Bible says, in 2 Corinthians 5:7 We have to walk by faith not by sight. One of the ways to walk with God is by having faith when we say our prayers or pray.

6. The sixth hindrance to our prayers is **not having pity or sympathy for the poor.** Proverbs 21:13 tells us that if a man shuts his ears to the cry of the poor, he too will cry out and not be heard and answered by God. We have to be ready to help the poor when we are asked or see them suffering, whether this is physical, emotional or spiritual. We are also told in Psalms 41:1-20 blessed is he who considers the poor; the Lord will deliver him in time of trouble. The Lord will also preserve and keep him alive. Furthermore, the Lord will bless him on the earth and will not deliver him to the will of his enemies. We have to be ready to have a giving and caring heart towards the poor, by devoting our time, prayers, resources and money. In so doing the Lord hears our prayers and petitions. He will not only protect and deliver us in times of trouble but would moreover pour out His blessing over us.

7. Another reason why our prayers are hindered is **because we do not pay attention to God's words.** The Lord God spoke through Zachariah when the people of Israel refused to pay attention. Stubbornly, they turned their backs and blocked their ears so that they would not hear. They also made their heart as hard as flint and would not listen to the law or to the words of the Lord Almighty. So the Lord Almighty became very angry with them and a great wrath came from Him because (He) had called but they did not listen, as had been predicted, saying: "when they call He (God) will not listen" (Zechariah 7:11-13).

8. The eighth hindrance to our prayers **is asking amiss or asking with a wrong motive.** James 4:3 reminds us that "You do not have because you do not ask God". When you ask, you do not receive because you ask with wrong motives, that you may spend what you get on your pleasures or lust. God's intention for us is that whatever we ask and receive from Him is with a good motive and that we use it for His purposes, to honour Him and give Him glory.

9. Unresolved conflicts or wrong human relationships are another hinderance to our prayers. If there are unresolved issues between two people, especially husband and wife, then this should be resolved before coming to God in prayer or otherwise, it would hinder the effectiveness of your prayers. There is the possibility that the husband or wife's prayers might be hindered. There is no point praying if you are fighting or having misunderstanding with each other. Apostle Peter in 1 Peter 3:7 states that "Husbands ... be considerate as you live with your wives, and treat them with respect as the weaker partner, and as heirs with you of the gracious gift of life, so that nothing will hinder your prayers". Our bad attitude, behaviour, bitterness, grudges towards a family member can hinder our prayers. Husbands, we have to live with our wives in an understanding way, with tender care, pursuing peace and honouring her. With regard to God answering our prayers, it is God's will that nothing blocks our relationship with Him and others. We should check/examine our hearts, actions and resolve any issues before we come to Him in confidence.

CHAPTER 13

FIFTEEN BASIC CONDITIONS FOR ANSWERED PRAYERS: ACHIEVING RESULTS

He shall call upon Me, and I will answer him

Psalm 91:15

It is estimated that out of the 667 prayers for specific things mentioned in the bible, there are 454 specific answers. That means that the Bible is a book of prayers and answers. The fact and the problem is that we spend a lot of time talking about prayer but fail to get down to the business or the art of praying. Prayer is never found on its own in the Bible. It's always mixed with something else. Prayer on its own is never enough to get God's answers. Once you learn how to mix your prayers with the things that activate them, your prayer will come alive. In the Bible, prayer is mixed with many different ingredients.

These are some of the keys for our prayers to be effectively answered by God.

1. We must pray from the heart for God to hear us. When we pray and seek the Lord with all our heart, He hears us (Jeremiah 29:12-13). When your heart is fully committed to the Lord, He hears and also strengthens you in all your ways (Jeremiah 30:21) The Lord answers those who devote themselves and draw close to him. God needs commitment and devotion of our heart when we seek him.

2. Pray with clean hands and a pure heart: For our prayers to be right and effective with God, we need to have clean hands (genuine activity) and a pure heart (character) to enter into the presence of God. Our pure heart has to be followed by a good action and the right motive. The Word of the Lord in Psalm 24:3-5 questions and earnestly asks "who may ascend the hill of the Lord? Who may stand in His holy place?" It also gave us the answer - "He who has a clean hand and a pure heart, who does not lift up his soul to an idol or swear by what is false". Anyone with clean hands, a pure heart, not lifting their soul to an idol or swear by what is false. We see that such a person will receive blessing and righteousness from the Lord and vindication from God his Saviour. I believe that to have your prayers answered, you must have the help of the Holy Spirit and pray with a pure heart, motive and your actions have to be right whenever you come to God's Presence through prayer.

3. Pray with vision: God's people cannot function without spiritual vision. This comes from revelation and brings certain hope. Vision stimulates faith, releases power and inspires action. Without spiritual sight, you cannot live the life of faith. This is why you must pray with sharp spiritual eyesight and insight. Sometimes you must pray with your eyes wide open! Bible say in (Proverbs 29:18) Where there is no vision my people perish. Faith operates by spiritual sight. Natural sight has nothing to do with this because (Hebrews 11:1) shows us that faith is the evidence of things which are not seen.

Everything which belongs to the spiritual realm is invisible to the natural eye. Indeed the realm of the Spirit cannot be grasped by any natural sense: not by seeing, touching, tasting, smelling or hearing. We do not look at the things which are seen, but at the things which are not seen. For the things which are seen is temporary but the things which are not seen are eternal. (2 Corinthians 4:18) This is why faith is vital for your earthly life. You would not need faith in heaven, for then you will see physically as well as spiritual. But for now, as a child of God, you have to live by faith. We see Jesus spiritually not physically, Jesus has not been revealed to us physically. Yet by faith, we already know him. Although we are waiting for the return of Jesus, we would see him face to face, (1John 3:2) we know and love him now.

We have to be aware that, spiritual vision comes before physical possession. After all, how can you pursue something unless you can see it clearly? Many people's lives are without vision. That is why they lack direction and miss God's purpose. It must be different for you- especially if you want to offer prayers that gets answers. If you 're going to take hold of God in prayer, you must have a faith- inspiring vision and this comes with with obedience for God to answer your prayers.

4. Pray with faith in the name of Jesus Christ: In the gospel of John, Chapter 14:13-14, Jesus assures us that God will do whatever we ask in His name so that He may bring glory to the Father. Jesus also emphasises again, in verse 14, that we may ask anything in His name, and He will do it. It's the faith we inject in His name, that give us the confidence to receive from him. We need to have faith to believe that God is the rewarder of those who diligently seek him (Hebrew 11.6). Jesus spoke in Matthew 17:20 to his disciples when they came to him in private to find out why they could not drive a demon out. Jesus said, it was because they had so little faith. He continued to tell them that, if you have faith as small as a mustard seed, you can say to this mountain move here and it will move. Nothing will be impossible for you. In Mark 11:23-24 Jesus encourages us to have faith in God. We should not doubt God when praying in relation to anything. Whenever we pray we have to believe that we have received whatever we have prayed for and it will be ours. In Isaiah 65:24, the word of God encourages us that before we call, He will answer and while we are speaking, He will hear. Hebrews 11:1 states that faith is now and the assurance of things hoped for and faith moves God. It takes faith to move God.

Real faith comes from knowing the person and the principles of God himself.

5. Pray by humbling yourself and seeking God's face, and turn from your wicked ways.

In 2 Chronicles 7:11-15 The Lord appeared to King Solomon at night and assured him that his prayers has been heard, This is an answer to revelation in contrast to God's judgement in Chapter 6:26-27. However, If Solomon does not want the heavens to be shut so that there is no rain, or command locusts to devour the land of Israel or send plague among his people, in order words famine, disaster and disease among his people because they have sinned against God, which confirms Solomon's prayer in the presiding Chapter 6:1-26,-28, when dedicating the temple. The Lord reinforced and gave assurance to Solomon verse in (2 Chronicles 7:14-15) " if my people, who are called by my name, will humble themselves, pray and seek my face and turn from the wicked ways, then will I hear from heaven and forgive their sin and heal their land. Now my eyes will be open and my ears attentive to their prayers offered in this place". If the people of God want their prayers to be answered, God want us to come to him by humbling ourselves (showing low self esteem, letting go of ego ,) in His presence, This also can be done by fasting Isaiah 58, (self -denial, self - humbling, right priorities and dependence on God), Psalms 35:13, and 69:10, Communicating with God by the help of the Holy Spirit, fully devoting ourselve to find him, and turning from our wicked ways, renouncing sin, evil and repenting, then God will hear our prayers from heaven, forgive our sin and heal our heart and land.

6. Pray with patience, expectancy and with thanksgiving: Our expectant prayers demonstrate confidence in God's goodness. The Lord is good to those who wait for Him, to the one who seeks Him. It is good that a man should both hope for and quietly wait for the salvation of the Lord. (Lamentations 3:25-26). By putting our hope, in the Lord alone can bring answers to our prayers (Psalm 62:5).

The expectation of the righteous will not be cut off. The Lord expects us to pray to Him with regards to everything. Paul encourages us in Philippians 4:6-7 that we should not be anxious about anything, but in everything by prayer and petition, with thanksgiving, we should present our requests to God. Then the peace of God, which transcends all understanding will guard our hearts and minds in Jesus Christ. So instead of fretting, or talking about it to everyone but taking God out of it, or taking matters into our own hands. Pray about it and trust God regardless of the outcome, He will honour our faith and patience. Pray and ask God for everything you need, always giving thanks, and the answer will come in His timing. God appreciates thanksgiving for the things He has done.

7. Pray with an undivided heart. Do your best to come to God not double-minded, but with your mind and heart being alert and fixed on God and His power. For it says in James 1:6-8, we should ask Him (God) in faith, not wavering, for he that waver is like a wave of the sea, blown and tossed by the wind. For such a person should not think that he will receive anything from the Lord. A double-minded man is unstable in all his ways. God does not want your mind to be wandering but to be steadfast in Him in faith. Jesus encourages us, in Matthew 21:22 that, whatsoever you shall ask in prayer, believing, you will receive. This is after he reminded the disciple in verse 21 that if they have faith and do not doubt, they can do the impossible.

8. Pray with a forgiving heart and walk in love: When we pray, we need to forgive anyone that we hold anything against, in order that our Father in heaven may also forgive us our sins (Mark 11:25) and answer our prayers (Mathew 5:23-25). We may receive answers for our prayers if we forgive, release and reconcile in our heart with anyone who has sinned against us (Matthew 6:14). The Bible says we should "walk in love as Christ also has loved us and given himself to us" (Ephesians 5:2).

Not only our heart but also our mouth is a major part of our love walk with God and with others. God told the Israelites that the reason they were not getting answers to their prayers was because they were engaged in finger pointing and criticism even when fasting (Isaiah 58:7-10). Are you self-sabotaging your prayers? It is important to glorify God through the words you speak to others, as when you are praying. Bible says there is a direct link between having a critical, careless tongue, and not getting your prayers answered. How you treat others will determine how God treats you (Ephesians 6:7-8). You must stop oppressing those who work for you and treat them fairly. Endeavour to share your food with the hungry as well as those who are helpless, poor, and destitute. If you do these things, God will shed His own glorious light on you. He will hear you, your Godliness will lead you forward, and goodness will be a shield before you. And the glory of the Lord will protect you from behind. Then when you call, the Lord will answer. We fail to realise how much we can do for people by building them up with our words instead of tearing them down. We need to be more careful not to say things that tear them down. The Bible says 'the heart is deceitful above all things and beyond cure, who can understand it? (Jeremiah 17:9). What vibes are you putting out there among people? Are you eager to show God's love? We have to examine your hearts, motives and attitudes. How do we do that? Examine our tongues and what is coming out of our mouth. This would make us spiritually healthy and get our prayers to be in line with God's heart.

9. Pray in truth. Jesus reminds us in John 14:6, that He is the way, truth and life. We need to pray in truth as He is the truth and his word is the truth. Jesus also before his arrest (John 17:1-3, 17), prayed for himself and for his disciples, that the Father in heaven should sanctify them by the truth; God's word is the truth. Psalm 145:18-19 encourages us that "the Lord is near to all who call on him and to all who call Him in truth". He fulfils the desires of those who fear Him. He hears their cry and saves them.

10. Pray in line with God's word and purposes: Pray according to what is written in God's word, locate where it is written according to the issue of your heart and pray it for the situation that you are in which requires change. The bible tells us in Isaiah 41:21 to present our case and set forth our arguments. This has to be aligned with God's word. Paul stated in 2 Timothy 2:13 that if we are faithless, God will remain faithful, for He cannot disown Himself. You must pray and take hold of His promises and purposes according to what God's word says in his manual - The Bible. The Bible says in 1 John 5:14 that "This is the confidence that we have in approaching God, that if we ask anything according to His will, He hears us."

His Word is His Will and the final authority. In Psalm 119:89 we read "Your word, O Lord is eternal, it stands firm in the heavens". Whatever we pray for we have to have confidence that it is according to God's written word.

11. Pray in the Spirit. We are to pray in the Spirit in order to connect with God. It is written in John 4:24 that God is a Spirit and those who worship Him must worship him in Spirit and Truth. You cannot pray effectively when you are walking in the flesh, carnality or its works as listed in Galatians 6:19. You need to repent of your sinfulness. Since our mind is carnal, we must live by the Spirit, pray in the Sprit and keep in step with the Spirit. If we do, our prayers would be much more effective as we are connected with God in humility and purity.

We are also encouraged in Jude 20 that we should build ourselves up in our most holy faith and pray in the Holy Spirit. In Ephesians 6:18 Paul strongly emphasises that Christians should pray in he Spirit on all occasions, with all kinds of prayers and requests. We need to have the desire to speak and pray to God more, using the gift of diverse kinds of tongues (1 Corinthians 12:10). Paul also encourages us in 1 Corinthians 14:2 that, anyone who speaks in a tongue does not speak to men but to God, as indeed, no-one understands him but the person praying utters mysteries with his Spirit.

12. Pray according to God's will and in submission to Him: When we pray in line with the word of God, we pray according to the will of God. When we let the word of God engineer our prayer, (1 John 5:14-15) we have the confidence, that if we ask anything according to His will he hear us. And if we know that He hears us, whatever we ask, we know that we have the petitions that we have asked of Him. Prayer based on the word of God result in answers but not on the problem. Since we sometimes pray, outside God's will, part of the Holy Spirit's job is to change our mind, and not convince God to give us what we want. This is why the Spirit searches our hearts in prayer. Sometimes words are inadequate. You do not always know what someone is really thinking or wants based on what they say. However if you could see inside their heart, you would know exactly how to interpret their words. This is what the Spirit does when He searches our hearts and interprets our requests to the Father (Romans 8:27). If the Holy Spirit is going to intercede for us (appeal to God on our behalf), we should better learn what God's will is. Where do we learn that? We learn that in His Word. Before we can pray in the will of God, three things need to happen.

Firstly, we must have a regular intake of scripture or God's word to understand the mind of God with the help of the Holy Spirit residing in our heart. God's mind is revealed in His word so that when you read the Bible you learn how to pray the way you should.

Secondly, if our prayers are going to hit the mark we need to practice meditating on the scriptures. By this I mean pondering on God's word in our hearts and minds so that it becomes part of us. We can then apply the known or meditated word of God to our situations, by the help of the Holy Spirit. When that happens, we will start to see things change in our prayer life because the Spirit's intercession is in line with God's will and His word. In so doing, God looks upon His word to perform it (Jeremiah 1:12). We need to have confidence when approaching the throne room of grace, so that we may receive mercy and find grace to help us in our time of need (Hebrew 4:16). We need to be assured that the confidence we have in approaching God is that if we ask anything according to His will, He hears us (1 John 5:14).

Thirdly, our prayers and requests must be in harmony with God's will. Jeremiah said 'The Lord is good to those who wait expectantly for Him (Lamentations 3:25). Expectant prayers demonstrate confidence in God's goodness. Also in Jeremiah 33:3 the Bible promised us that we should call on Him (God) and He will answer us by showing us great and unsearchable things that we do not know. God's known will is what He has revealed to us in His Word. His unknown will is what is not written in His word but what He reveals to us in our inner spirit.

13. Open your ears to hear the cry of the poor: Be attentive and listen to the cry of the poor. Share your time, resources, finances and strength with them by having a giving and caring heart (Proverbs 21:13, Isaiah 58:7, Matthew 25:35-36 Psalm 41:1-2). In Isaiah 58 the Lord explains to us what true fasting is and tells us some of the things that we can do to the poor for our prayer to be answered. (Isaiah 58:7-10) Paraphrase "You must stop oppressing those who work for you and treat them fairly. We have to share our food with the hungry and to help those who are helpless, poor, and destitute, if you do these things, God will shed His own glorious light on you. He will hear you, your godliness will lead you forward, and goodness will be a shield before you. You will receive healing and the glory of the Lord will protect you from behind. Then, when you call, the Lord will answer you and say "Here I am".

14. Pay attention to God with your heart, mind and listen to Him with your inner spirit: We have to connect with God with our new regenerated heart, a pure heart without any sinfulness and a renewed mind through the word of God. We should be able to listen to Him and then when we call He will answer (Jeremiah 33:3, Romans 12:2, John 14:14, Zachariah 7:11-13). We need to rest and wait on God patiently Psalm (37:7).

15. Pray in the name of the Lord Jesus: We need to pray using the name of Jesus. Through Jesus we have access to the Father. Jesus has given us the authority to use his name when communicating or praying to the Father. In John 14:13-14 Jesus confirmed that "I will do whatever you ask in my name, so that the son may bring glory to the Father". In verse 14 of John 14, Jesus continues to say "that you may ask for anything in my name and I will do it". In the Gospel of John Chapters 14, 15, and 16, Jesus tells his disciples what they can do if they do it in his name. He has also given us his name to drive out demons when we pray (Mark 16:17). In the book of Acts, the disciples used the name of Jesus when praying to drive out demons, to heal the sick and also when performing various miracles by the power of God. To pray in his name is to pray as Jesus prayed and to pray to the father as Jesus makes Him known. There is power in the name of Jesus (Philippians 2:10) and at the name of Jesus, every knee will bow in heaven and on earth and under the earth and every tongue will confess that he is Lord to the glory of God.

God is calling us to come to him so that He can reason with us. Even though our sins are like scarlet, they shall be as white as snow, though they are red as crimson, they shall be as white as wool (Isaiah 1:18). God cannot wait for us to come to Him in order for us to reason and communicate together. He is ever waiting. He wants us to draw near to him, and he will then draw near to us (James 4:8). God wants our prayers to be set before Him like a sweet smelling incense, similar to what David prayed and sang in Psalm 141:2 "May my prayer be set before you like incense, May the lifting up of my hands be like the evening sacrifice".

16. Pray exercising all your God given authority against satanic forces:

Jesus in Luke 9:1 gave the twelve disciples power and authority to drive out all demons and to cure all diseases. We are confident that when we pray, we have authority given in Jesus's name and power through the Holy Spirit to cast out all demonic activities and to cure diseases. We also have this authority and power when we pray and involve ourselves in evangelism. Bearing in mind that Jesus has disarmed all powers and authorities, and made a public spectacle of the Devil, triumphing over evil by the Cross. This is demonstrated in Luke 10:17 when the demons were subjected to the seventy disciples in the name of Jesus. The victory belongs to God and Christians and Jesus always wins.

17. God answers our prayers according to the power that Christ is at work in us. Paul in Ephesians 3:19-20 tells us that the 'Christ working power' that is at work in us enables us to pray effectively.

FOUR WAYS GOD ANSWERS PRAYER:

I have come to believe there are 4 ways God answers prayers.

- Yes, the answer to have his approval.

Note: God will never answer Yes to any request that is contrary to the will of God - (the word of God).

If the answer is "Yes" and the question is contrary to the will of God (the authenticity and authority of the word of God), the answer is from you, not Him.

- No. Blatant no.
- Wait. It is not time.
- I have something better

CHAPTER 14

THE BENEFITS OF PRAYER

There are many benefits of prayer, but let's look at few of the benefits.

1. In prayer we meet God and get to know Him.

There is no better way to know God than to spend quality time with him each day. Prayer helps us to understand His word by the help of the Holy Spirit.

King David, towards the end of his life stood in front of his leaders, advisors and mighty men to advise his son Solomon. He said (1 Chronicles 28:9), "And you my son Solomon, acknowledge the God of your fathers, and serve Him with wholehearted devotion and with a willing mind, for the Lord searches every heart and understands every motive behind our thoughts. If you seek Him, He will be found by you, but if you forsake Him, He will reject you forever.

Yes, in prayer alone with Him, you get to know God in deeper relationship and intimacy. I do not think there is anything more important in our life than this.

Jesus said to Martha, only one thing is needed, and Mary has chosen that good part, which will not be taken from her. Luke 10:42 Hearing the Lord's teaching and prayer.

2. In prayer we are strengthened.

Through prayer and the word of God, we are strengthened to overcome the flesh, the world and the Devil. Let's consider these verses in Isaiah 40:29-31.

He gives strength to the weary, and increases the power of the weak. Even youths grow tired and weary, and young men stumble and fall, but those who hope in the Lord will renew their strength. They will soar on wings like eagles, they will run and not grow weary, and they will walk and not be faint.

In Luke 22:39-46: when Jesus was wrestling in prayer in the Garden of Gethsemane, he invited his disciples to pray with him, but his disciple did not join him but slept instead. This is a common problem with Christians. You can also find a full account of this (Matthew 26:36-46).

We notice in Luke 22:43, it was recorded that an angel from Heaven appeared to Jesus and strengthened him.

There are many scriptures to confirm that God strengthens us when we interact with Him in prayer.

3. Through prayer, we receive revelation, guidance and direction.

Prayer can change our day, our attitude, our heart condition, how we view our circumstances and it can give us direction and lead to success in our life.

Daniel, John and Paul, to name but a few, received revelation and direction from God through their prayers. As I mentioned in a previous chapter, Paul as a man of prayer (Acts 16:9), receives a vision during the night of a Macedonian man standing and begging, " come over to Macedonia and help us". After Paul have seen the vision, they got ready at once to leave for Macedonia, concluding that God had called them to preach the gospel there.

Daniel also, as a man of prayer, received revelation, direction and interpretation of dreams for Nebuchadnezzar and his kingdom, nations and for Daniel himself (Daniel Chapters 1 to 12).

4. Through prayer our faith is quickened.

Through prayer our faith and that of others can be quickened, stirred and increased. Jesus is the author and finisher of our faith.

Faith does not come by hearing the word of God alone, but also spending time with the word of God Jesus (John 1:1-4).

In Hebrews 12:2, we are told to run the race with endurance,

"Looking unto Jesus is the author and finisher of our faith."

When we spend time with him, our faith is enlarged, built up, strengthened and quickened.

"And the Lord said, Simon, Simon, Satan has asked to sift you as wheat. But I have prayed for you, Simon that your faith may not fail. And when you have returned, strengthen your brothers".

Here, Peter's faith was strengthened through Jesus prayers. We too can pray in the same way for ourselves and others.

5. Through prayer we are helped to overcome temptation.

In Matthew 26:40-41 when Jesus was praying in the Garden of Gethsemane prior to his arrest, he reminded his disciples several times to watch and pray. While finding them sleeping, he asked them a question; could you not keep watch with me for one hour? He asked Peter in verse 41 Jesus reaffirmed to the disciples, "Watch and pray so that you will not fall into temptation". The disciples didn't "watch and pray" and subsequently entered into temptation, they ran off and deserted Jesus. Prayer is a spiritual activity, it needs decision and commitment. The flesh is weak and would rather sleep or watch too much television. When we watch and pray, it helps us not to fall into temptation. Prayer helps and strengthens us in time of temptation. It give us encouragement and confidence when facing troubles (2 Corinthians 10.11).

6. Through prayers we receive peace.

"Do not be anxious about anything, but in everything by prayer and petition, and with thanksgiving, present your requests to God. And the peace of God which transcends all understanding will guard your hearts and your minds in Jesus Christ" (Philippians 4:6-7). Prayer is a shield against our anxiety and worry.

A God given restful peace, which passes all understanding, comes to us when we pray. As I have said before there are many benefits to prayer, through prayers we have victory, provision, confidence, healing, power and breakthrough. When we neglect prayers it is to our peril. God legally does not demand our prayers but when we pray we are the ones who benefit.

7. Through prayers we produce an atmosphere of power.

In the book of Acts 2:14-41, during and after the disciples had prayed, it was recorded that the glory of God broke through with the disciples and signs, wonders and salvation followed them. After Peter had preached the word of God, this resulted in the addition of 3,000 souls who believed, were baptised and then added to the church. There are many answered prayers that have been recorded in the Bible and mentioned in previous chapters in this book through God's power. Prayer allows us to affect the life of anyone in the world.

8. Prayer is the method by which God provides our needs.

God has promised in His word that, we should ask and we would receive (Luke 11: 9-12) and also He will provide all our needs according to His riches in Christ Jesus (Philippians 4:19). So, we use prayer as a means to ask of our request, Even though God knows our needs (Matthew 6:32) He wants us to ask.

9. Prayer is a source of healing, both emotional and physical to our body.

Purposeful prayers help us to have healing to our physical body. Jesus in his early years of ministry healed a lot of people. To name a few, the healing of a demon - possessed man (Mark 5:1-20), the man with leprosy was cured in Mark 1:40-45, the woman with the issue of blood (Mark 5:21-34). Jesus did all these, with the anointing in his life and also having prayed prior to these healings. Paul reminds us in James 5:14-16 Paraphrase "if anyone is sick among the believers they should call the elders of the church to pray over them and anoint them with oil in the name of Jesus and the prayer offered in faith will make the sick person whole (Act 3:1-10). Peter and John healed the crippled beggar at the temple gate called Beautiful. They had prayed prior to this and the crippled man was healed and praised God.

CHAPTER 15

THE THREE SPIRITUAL DIMENSIONS THAT GOD ANSWERS PRAYERS

1. In the dimension of human will:

God uses human will to answer our prayers (Acts 9:10-19). The Lord Jesus used Ananias as part of the answer to the prayers of the Lord's disciples against the murderous treats by Saul of Tarsus. Sometimes somebody's decision is determined by someone else. Human beings are used as a vehicle either for your prayers not to be answered or to be answered. God can use dreams, visions, prophecy, inner intuition, His Word, and by the gifts of the Holy Spirit.

2. The angelic dimension:

In Daniel 9 &10, we are told how an angel of the Lord appeared to Daniel in a vision to reveal answers and mysteries after he had prayed and fasted with regards to the desolation of Jerusalem. During Jesus prayers in the Garden of Gethsemane, (Luke 22:39-45) an angel from heaven appeared to him and strengthened him.   Sometimes God uses angels (Hebrew 1:14, Acts 5:19, Act 12:7) to brings answers to our prayers. There are ministering angels who minister to us.

3. In the dimension of God's Sovereign Will.

This is where God does not need humans, angels or His own command. He answers or does whatever pleases Him, because He is a sovereign God who rules the heavens and the earth.

Our problem is not that God is saying a loving no to many of our requests, it is that our prayers too often lack the depth that heaven requires. They seem to come from the head, not the heart. Instead of being propelled from our spirit towards God with earnestness and faith that can not be denied. They often wobble from uncertain lips and fall helpless to the father.

Will you take up this challenge of prayer and be connected with God? If you do, you will see the mighty hand of God move in your life, your family, your workplace, your church and your nation. May the men of prayer arise, may the women of prayer arise, we have to pray as individuals, we have to pray as a family, we have to pray as a nation, we have to pray as Christians, we have to pray as a Church because prayer works and is relevant.

I believe that when we pray, our prayers ascend to and are reserved in heaven in a vial before God's throne. In Revelation 5:8, when He had taken the book, the four living creatures and twenty-four elders fell down before the lamb. Every one of them had harps and golden bowls full of incense, which are the prayers of the Saints. God releases the answers to our prayers whenever it pleases him according to his own timing. Our prayers also are a memorial to us in heaven. Acts 10:1-4 shows us this in relation to Cornelius's regular generous giving and offering of prayers by being a righteous person by the grace of God. An angel of the Lord who had a golden censer, came and stood at the altar of the Lord. He was given much incense to offer, **with the prayers of all the Saints presented on the golden altar before the throne**. The smoke of the incense, **together with the prayers of the Saints** went up before God from the angel's hand (Revelation 8:3-4).

I firmly believe that when we get to heaven, we'll see countless rewards given to people who never preached from a platform, who were never identified as great leaders, but who prayed faithfully without fail.

All who are faithful in this discipline of prayer shall be rewarded in the future. Whoever continues in this kind of labour in secret will not go unrewarded. May God raise up people to pray for His work.

I believe that this book will widen your spiritual perspective, deepen and broaden your horizons in your personal and family prayer life, and improve your church prayer life. It is my prayer that God, Who is able to do exceedingly abundantly above what we ask or think according to the power that is at work within us, will bless you. May God help you to have the necessary desire and discipline to make your prayer life a delight. May you be a blessing to others, in Jesus's name and if you have been blessed by this book please do pass it on to somebody.

BIBLIOGRAPHY

Scripture quotations from NIV. NEW INTERNATIONAL VERSION 1984

Scripture quotations from THE RAINBOW STUDY BIBLE: King James Version copyright 1981 1986 1989 and 1992

Scripture quotations from THE HEBREW-GREEK KEY STUDY BIBLE King James Version 1991

THE HANDY BIBLE DICTIONARY & CONCORDANCE 1983

NEW CONCISE BIBLE DICTIONARY A-Z 1989

NEW BIBLE COMMENTARY 21ST CENTURY EDITION copyright C 1973 1978 1984

VINES COMPLETE EXPOSITORY DICTIONARY OF OLD & NEW TESTAMENT WORDS copyright 1978

DR. LEA LARRY: COULD YOU NOT TARRY ONE HOUR? Notes on the model of the Lord's Prayer 1987

THE POWERFUL LIFE OF GEORGE MULLER OF BRISTOL by Clive Laymad- Published by CWR ISBN: 1-85345391-1

BIBLE ENCYCLOPEDIA